AUTHENTIC YOU.

A Girl's Guide to Growing Up Fearless and True

ACHEA REDD

D1205623

WISE INK

ISBN 13: 978-1-63489-361-9
Library of Congress Catalog Number: 2020915235

Printed in the United States of America
First Printing: 2021

25   24   23   22   21   5   4   3   2   1

Cover design by Luke Bird

Wise Ink Creative Publishing
807 Broadway St NE, Suite 46
Minneapolis, MN, 55413

To order, visit www.itascabooks.com or call
1-800-901-3480. Reseller discounts available.

CONTENTS

Chapter One

WELCOME TO CHANGE

In many ways, adolescence feels like life as usual. Change happens really slowly, and often in ways we don't expect. Life is a series of constant, gradual stages of transition, and you're in the middle of a big one right now. Many people don't realize how much they've changed until they look back in time. That makes sense, because we often see our past selves much more clearly than we see ourselves in the moment.

I wrote this book as a guide for you, because things are changing, and change is always disruptive. In fact, it might suck.

You've probably heard a lot of people (mostly parents and teachers) talk about adolescence like it's the worst and most difficult thing. Like you'll spend years freaking out about how your body is changing, screaming at your parents, or staying out until the early morning at crazy parties only to come home and get grounded within an inch of your life. But while it's true that you're undergoing huge changes as a person, and you may be becoming someone your parents don't recognize, your life isn't a stereotype. It's uniquely yours, and that makes it hard to navigate.

I wrote this book because there were things I wished I knew growing up that could have helped me feel more confident then. I didn't want to be told how to act or respond to what was coming at me in life, but I did wish I'd been warned more about what to expect when my life changed as I got older. I have anxiety—which means I worry a lot about things that might happen—and I wanted to be more prepared for how to deal with growth and change in my life. In the years ahead, you'll get to decide which parts of yourself you want to grow, which parts you want to stay the same, and which parts you're ready to leave behind. I hope this book helps you approach those choices fearlessly.

In my life now (though I *wish* I had it when I was

younger), I and thousands of other women live by a simple mantra: **Real Girls FART.** Sounds silly at first, I know. After all, why would I put farting in a book as a good thing? But the truth is that, to be happy, we have to accept the parts of ourselves that we don't usually share with the world, and FART is an acronym that helps us remember this.

I've spent my whole life struggling to be *real*. To be the person I believe I am on the inside, on the outside. And I've figured out that people are able to be their truest, kindest, best selves when they're **F**earless and **A**uthentic and when they're **R**escuers and **T**railblazers. In everything you do, in all the choices you make, ask yourself if you're living up to your *real* potential.

Is your life controlled by the fear of what people will think of you? Are you doing the things you like and that make you happy, rather than what everyone else is doing? Are you advocating for yourself and supporting the people around you? Are you willing to lead, to be up in the front, helping others to be brave?

In each of these chapters, we'll go through topics such as friends, romance, and responsibility; and we'll outline exactly what it means to embody the Real Girls FART mentality. Each section will have an affirmation that you can repeat to yourself quietly to remind you who you are, or to shout from the rooftops for all to hear.

Embrace this middle space of your life called transition. It's uncomfortable, yes. But without it, you'll never get to meet who you'll become on the other side. You are wonderful, real girl. I'm so excited to welcome you to this sisterhood.

I AM FEARLESS.
I am powerful beyond measure.

Even though you're at an "important" age, it doesn't necessarily mean everything you do needs to be serious and failproof. Right now is a great time to experiment with the things you think are interesting.

This is a time of openness and creativity. In this moment, you have way more power than you ever had before, and you get to use it to do the things you think are meaningful and that make you laugh.

Embrace your freedom, and lean into the new

experiences that excite you. Do new creative projects, explore the area around where you live, and join after-school activities that spark your interest. Don't be afraid to talk to people you think seem cool and interesting, and don't worry about impressing anyone. Trust your instincts and that little inner voice that's telling you who you're meant to be and what you're meant to do.

For lots of people, this is a time of high energy and of doing what you want just because you want to. Although this can get you into trouble, it's also a great recipe for adventure and independence—and it's a lot of fun!

Even if you make missteps along the way, you have *so much* power over your life and your mind. You have the drive and the passion to set the stage for what your life will be like. Don't let anyone else's idea of who you should be get in the way of what you know is possible for yourself!

I AM AUTHENTIC.

I will become who I want to be.

Life right now is filled with intense emotional moments. Not even considering how stressful school is, you're probably dealing with bullies, friendships and relationships, trends, jealousy, and all the drama that comes with those. It's easy to be cruel to someone, and it's even easier to take someone else's cruelty to heart.

Sometimes the pressure to think and act in a certain way can be overwhelming. I should know. I grew up a pastor's kid, so anything I did or thought that didn't match what was accepted in the church wasn't allowed, and I often felt like a disappointment.

I've also seen people—adults, even—completely change who they are in order to impress people they admire. It makes them hard to trust. More importantly, if you pretend to be something you're not, you might forget who you really are.

Of course, the pressure to find your *true* self can seem as intense as social pressure. After all, who can really say they'll never change? Change is good if it's authentic. So give yourself a break. As long as you aren't doing anything that makes you feel bad about yourself, it's okay to try on different personalities and different looks. It's even okay to hang out with different friend groups. It's all part of figuring out what feels good to you and what doesn't.

So go explore! After all, is there a better time than right now to dye your hair blue, hang out at your friend's house and blast some music, or pull a harmless prank on one of your parents? Experiment in a way that makes you feel free, positive, and creative.

I AM A RESCUER.

I will be gentle with myself.

Even if you aren't a rebellious teen who skateboards through life on unnecessary risks and parental disapproval, you'll still find you have many moments of conflict and emotional pain. Most people can think of really bad fights they had with their friends during middle school and high school, or disagreements with their parents that escalated quickly.

While it's fine to spend time stewing in some good old-fashioned emotional turmoil, know that these feelings are perfectly normal. They don't mean there's anything wrong with you. Crying doesn't mean you can't cope, or that this one fight is going to impact your life in some deep, dark way.

Being kind to yourself is the best way to get through these moments. If your friend is having a hard time, you wouldn't slap them to make them feel better. So don't add fuel to the fire by being overly critical of yourself. You can only make yourself and others feel better by giving them compassion and space to heal. Let yourself cry, scream, and take a break from the world, and then take a deep breath.

Even when you're lying awake at night thinking about something embarrassing you said or did the day before, know that it will pass. In a few days, weeks, or months, people won't even remember that it happened. Everyone has their own life to keep up with—people aren't going to spend eons remembering your flaws, and good friends won't care. So be gentle with yourself. You deserve it.

I AM A TRAILBLAZER.

I won't compare my journey to anyone else's.

Everyone grows at a different pace. Just because one girl has a killer Instagram profile doesn't mean you need to let jealousy take over. Just because someone seems like they have everything together doesn't mean they do. And even if they *do* have everything together, it doesn't mean you are hopeless or should feel bad for not being perfect all the time. Comparison doesn't make anyone feel better.

If your life right now is all about freedom and options, know that nobody's journey is going to look just like anyone else's. The things you go through, think about, and deal with are separate from other people's issues. It's important to face each issue in your life head-on at your own pace and at the right time.

If you think about the people you admire most, they probably aren't hung up on what other people are doing. They're thinking about what *they* want to do and how to do it. You're also only seeing their successes, not their mistakes. So remember that you don't need to get it right the first time!

Your path will never be the same as those of the people you admire, but you can use theirs as inspiration to think about the things that matter most to you. You can use their examples to strengthen your inner compass, which will point you in the direction of your unique path.

So go forth, experiment, have fun, and remember not to take yourself too seriously. Remember that things will change, and that's perfectly okay. Change is an opportunity to build something real for yourself, an identity and value system that will form the basis for all the things you're doing and becoming. This is your moment, so take it and shine.

Chapter Two

FRIENDS

When you think of your best friends, each one is probably "best" to you for a different reason. Maybe one always likes your selfies and boosts your confidence. Maybe another is your favorite person to do homework with. Or maybe you have a whole crew who you can just be yourself around. In all these situations, these friends are people who make you feel good about yourself.

It's easy, though, to get stuck in "friendships" that aren't friendly at all. Maybe we don't think we deserve better (but we do!), or maybe our world is just too small and we haven't met our true people yet. When I was a teenager, that was exactly what my life looked like.

Back then, I went to a small, private Christian

school, and everything about it was exactly like what you see on TV. The rules were strict, the student body was tiny, we wore uniforms every day, and I felt like there was nowhere I could go to be my real self. And just like in every movie about mean girls in high school, I belonged to a clique of three girls, and they made my life miserable. They were always pointing out my flaws—how I sounded when I talked, the way my body was shaped, the way my hair looked— and it really grated on me.

When you grow up seeing the same people day after day for your whole life, you know it isn't easy to replace bad friends with good ones. It feels like everyone else at school is already taken, or you know them well enough by now that you just aren't interested in being friends.

Things get worse when your friends make your life hell, even when you aren't friends anymore. In our clique, my friends and I were tightly connected in a dysfunctional way. Whenever I tried to break off from the group to get a break from the drama, the ringleader of the group would turn everyone else at school against me.

She had power over me no matter where I went,

and I felt trapped. Under her thumb, I couldn't grow as a person. I couldn't be who I wanted to be. It wasn't until the summer I turned sixteen that I met my first real best friend and discovered what true friendship really looked like. She embraced everything about me as I was, even as I gradually changed into the best version of myself. With my first real friend, I suddenly knew I could do anything. And from there, I never looked back.

Female relationships are complex. There's no one single solution for dealing with conflict among your friends—we all have to struggle through it as part of growing up. The more we experience conflict, though, the better we get at dealing with it. But it does get better, I promise you. And you might just come out the other side stronger than you were before.

I AM FEARLESS.

I can do anything with my friends by my side.

Okay, maybe having friends doesn't always make you feel that invincible. The world outside your comfort zone is full of terrifying unknowns and the risk of failure. Regardless of how many people are cheering you on from the sidelines, you're not sure you can do it by yourself.

When you're filled with self-doubt, that's exactly the right time to team up with a friend to try something new together. Just like the African proverb "Sticks in a bundle can't be broken," you're more likely to have fun when you try a new thing with someone else instead of doing it alone.

Think of some new things you want to try that scare you, like joining the school musical or basketball team, starting a band, or taking an advanced math class. Doing things outside your comfort zone with a friend makes them more fun and way less scary. Sometimes the fact that something scares you might mean that it's a good thing for you to try. It's okay to feel nervous when you branch out like that. Those nerves are a sign that you're pushing the boundaries of your comfort zone and growing as a person.

We fear trying something new because we don't know beforehand if we'll be good at it. You and your friends each have special skills you bring to the table when you're doing a new activity for the first time, so imagine what would happen if you combined them. Friends make us stronger. When we spend enough time together, their good qualities (like their passions and skills) start to rub off on us. Soon we become better, more skilled people too. Spend enough time practicing and learning from each other, and pretty soon you'll be an unstoppable team.

Of course, sometimes you can't do *everything* together. You're lucky if you find someone in your life you have everything in common with. But more often than not, being different from your friends is good for you. So even if your friend doesn't always want to do the same activities, ask them to come watch you audition or practice once in a while. In that way, they can be kind of like your sidekick. If your friends can't be right next to you on the field, invite them to watch from the sidelines. You can't expect them to be there every time, but when they do show up, you'll feel stronger by knowing you aren't alone.

Trying something new with a friend you already have makes the process less intimidating. But what if you can't find a friend to do it with you? That doesn't mean your existing friends are bad, but it does mean you have the opportunity to meet new people. New activities equal new friends, plain and simple. There are probably plenty of cool new people on the volleyball team or student council you'll get along with; you just don't know it yet. Never stop yourself from doing something you think you may love just because you're afraid of doing it alone.

When I turned sixteen, I was really lonely. I was hoping that when the upcoming school year started, I'd finally be free of my mean friends. But I didn't know what I could do in my power to make that happen. Everything changed that summer when I started my first job at the Finish Line shoe store at the mall in my hometown.

I was excited about the job—I couldn't wait to start earning my own money, and I loved that I'd get to spend all day at the mall. But I was also nervous. I'd never had a job before, and I was shy and didn't know how to interact with customers. Starting my first-ever job by myself felt like being pushed out of my comfort zone a little too fast, like squeezing too much toothpaste out of the tube.

At first, anyway. Not long after I started, I met my

coworker Natasha. She would show up wearing the coolest clothes and sneakers, and she always seemed at ease around the customers. Natasha had already been working at the store for a while, and whenever we worked the same shifts, I found myself looking up to her for guidance in how to act and handle tough situations with customers. She was so patient and willing to train me into the job, and little did she realize that her kindness was helping me find another side of myself.

We spent so much time together at and outside of work that we quickly became best friends—my first best friend!—even though she went to a different school. She never judged me, and she was the first person I felt like I could truly be myself around. I finally had freedom, and I could feel myself starting to change into the person I had always wanted to be. It's not that I was comparing myself to Natasha and trying to be like her when we were together. It was that being around someone who was kind and supportive helped me be more like myself in the first place.

Soon enough, I was hanging out with Natasha's other friends too, and I felt like I finally belonged somewhere. My social circle completely flipped in the course of a couple short months. I wasn't totally free of my mean girl clique when school started again that fall, but knowing I had true friends waiting for me outside of school made it so much more bearable. I had compartmentalized my relationships between school friends and true friends, and the benefits leaked into every part of my life. My grades started going up, and I was an even better employee at work—all because I had stepped out of my comfort zone a few months earlier.

We tend to think of friends as fun people to do things with, but your friends are also your support network. Big, terrifying life events can come out of nowhere and make you feel like you need your friends more than ever. Maybe your parents are divorcing, and you need a friend whose house you can escape to when things are chaotic at home. Maybe you got your first period, and it's easier to ask your friend instead of your mom about how tampons work. Maybe you're going through your first breakup, and you need someone to listen to you when you're sad.

These are normal parts of life changing as you grow up. Just because they're normal doesn't mean they aren't hard! It does mean you aren't the only one going through them, though. When you feel like you don't have control over something in your life that's changing, friends can make you feel less alone or give you the support you aren't getting anywhere else. With my best friend Natasha, for example, my mom and I became her support network. Natasha didn't have a great relationship with her own mom when she needed it the most, so she became close to mine. The closer we became as friends, the more she felt like a sister to me, like we were there for each other no matter what.

You can't stop yourself from growing up, but friends can make the process feel a little more normal. And once you've assembled your friends into a support network, maybe you *will* start feeling a little more invincible after all.

I AM AUTHENTIC.

I will not change to be who others want me to be.

Sometimes we forget who we really are. I don't mean that in the amnesia sense—I mean that, as girls, the world is always telling us to be someone else, our parents are telling us to be someone else, and our friends are telling us to be someone else too. We inhale and swallow everyone else's insecurities and issues as our own, and we start to think that the problem is us, not them.

Online, there's no escape from the pressure. Celebrities post pictures of themselves looking thin, beautiful, and flawless. What we don't think about is the stylist who did their makeup (it takes a LOT of makeup to get that "no-makeup" look) or the photo filter that lightened their skin and smoothed the dimples on their thighs. What we think about instead is this: *Why can't I be that perfect?*

The truth is, you already are. Being your true, authentic self is better than being a fake version of a million other people, no matter how richer, prettier, or thinner they might look on Instagram.

We grow up hearing all this noise about who we should become, and the self-hate it breeds within us makes us forget who we already are. We forget that we don't have to change to be worth something. When we're constantly hating and hiding our true selves, it can be hard to find friends who bring out the best in us by loving us for who we are. Instead of becoming friends based on lifting each other up (what we really need), we build our friendships on a foundation of tearing each other down.

I struggled with this a lot when I was younger. Even outside my clique of mean girls at school, I was bullied for the color of my skin and for the way my hair looked. People called me Pancake Butt because my butt was flat, but at the same time I was convinced I was fat. I felt like I was constantly falling short of how other people wanted me to be, and I became very defensive around other girls. The friendships I made back then weren't the kind that made me feel better about myself—they just fueled my inner fire of self-hate, making me feel worse and worse.

The world teaches us to hate ourselves because it's afraid of the power we would have if we loved ourselves instead. It also teaches us to hate other girls because it's truly afraid of what we could do if we recognized our power together. All those new, fun, scary things you can do with friends become a lot harder when you're grappling with hate from others and from yourself. To fix the problem, we have to redefine what it means to be beautiful.

Defining Your Standard of Beauty

Girls can be powerful in every way possible, but those who define what the world sees as beautiful mainly exist in the media, whether that's fashion, music, or film. The world looks to them for the latest standard of beauty, and for centuries, that has looked a lot like what we just talked about: thin, white, rich, straight, and hidden under layers of makeup. Even though the standard is slightly shifting, more often it feels like all the women we see online or on TV today were created from the same mold.

The mold wasn't made to fit us, but the good news is that you're still beautiful anyway. I know, I know—it's one thing to be told you're beautiful, and it's another thing entirely to actually believe it and love yourself for who you are. When it feels like the world doesn't love you back, loving yourself in spite of that becomes an act of resistance. It makes you the leader of a revolution.

In order to make room in the world for you to love yourself, you have to redefine what beauty means to you. Start with these three steps:

1. Stop comparing yourself to other people. It seems like other people always have it better than us, don't they? They have less acne, flatter bellies, better hair—the list goes on. Wanting what someone else has can make us hate what we *do* have. Comparing ourselves to other people breaks down our self-esteem, which makes us compare ourselves more, which makes our self-esteem even worse. It's an endless cycle.

If we stop looking at what we don't have (and probably never will have, at least not right now), we'll stop letting ourselves be influenced by unattainable images of beauty and perfection. All that time we spent looking at other people is now free time to look at ourselves. Suddenly we've freed up space inside for love to grow. The more we look at ourselves without anyone else to compare us to, eventually we'll forget why we even hated who we are in the first place.

2. Stop listening to other people. People love to not mind their own business. There's a saying that goes, "If you don't have anything nice to say, don't say it at all," and some people willfully ignore it as they make a point to tell you that you're too loud or your laugh sounds weird or your hair is too big. Whether they're talking about your looks or personality, comments or jokes like this make us feel self-conscious. Instead of making us love those parts of ourselves, we want to hide them from other people's attention.

People like this are mean. If they're your friends, I'd call them secret bullies. (More on that in a moment.) Their words make us want to change to get their approval. But even if we do, they'll keep putting us down because that's just who they are—and that creates a whole other cycle of poor self-esteem. We think that by trying to fix ourselves, we'll fix someone else into a nicer person. But that will never happen, and now we've ruined ourselves in the process.

The only approval in your life that matters is your own. If you find ways to shut out the opinions of people who can't mind their business (try whipping out phrases like "Let me live!" or "Stop judging me!"), you'll be self-affirming the way you are as the only way you know how to be. And that's what beauty looks like.

3. Embrace your quirks. The final step to learning to love your authentic self involves taking those things people comment on too often and using them for good. When you own your quirks, they turn out to be your greatest strengths. Not all of your quirks are problems that need to be solved.

Here's an example of a time I once struggled with embracing my quirks. I used to not realize I was an introvert, or someone who is naturally quieter. My friends who were louder and more social seemed to be the ones who got all the attention from boys, teachers, and other friends, and I felt pressure to be like that too. But every time I tried to act like my friends, I wasn't being my true self. I didn't realize that quieter people are just as valuable. We can be more creative, better listeners, and harder workers. The secret about being shy or an introvert is that we're just as great as extroverts, but we aren't always loud enough to make people notice it.

Once I started being more like myself, I saw that my friends still liked me. I was able to like them better too, because I wasn't trying to be like them. I finally accepted that I'm a quieter person, and I felt more real every time I did have the spotlight put on me because I had truly earned it. I wasn't faking who I was to get the attention—all my interactions with people became genuine. Owning my introversion made me a better friend and person.

Turn your quirks into strengths by refusing to apologize for them and by using them for good, whether for yourself or for other people. Your new strengths make it easier to stop comparing yourself to other girls too. They don't make you as jealous anymore, because you realize that you aren't meant to be exactly like them. When you embrace your quirks, you're no longer more or less strong, brilliant, or beautiful than someone else—you're just exactly who you need to be.

Friendship Boundaries

Friends can sometimes look a lot like that old sweater in our closet from last year: we love it so much, but it just doesn't fit anymore. We take for granted the fact that it's always in our closet, and we never stop to think about getting rid of it. We're used to it being there, and it brings up nice memories every time we look at it. But it just isn't serving us the way it used to.

Like our old clothes, it's important to try on old friendships from time to time to make sure our relationships aren't piling up with useless baggage. Growing apart from friends over time is natural, and it can happen without you even noticing. One day, *boom!* Things just don't feel right anymore. Your interests, class schedules, group of friends, or any number of factors have changed. When this happens, it's important to remember two things:

1. It's no one's fault that you and your friend have evolved into people who need different friendships.

2. You can't fix a friend back into whoever you want them to be.

Friendships have as much gray area as romantic relationships. There isn't always a clear-cut path as to whether you should keep a friend or move on. The solution can be simply setting boundaries with your friends and making sure you never lose sight of what you're worth in a friendship. Ultimately, what you and your friends need is a little room between yourselves so you can grow.

Just because things have gotten a little unhealthy doesn't mean your friendship can't be fixed. You don't have to cut people out of your life as soon as you sense they have changed—and change isn't always a bad thing. Boundaries aren't the same as walls. Your boundaries don't have to keep people out of your life altogether. They can just give you space when you need it. Sometimes this space looks like safety when people in your life are bad for you, but more often this space looks like giving yourself room to rediscover who you are.

When you're making boundaries for yourself, remember to put yourself first. It can be uncomfortable to do that—it makes us feel like a bad, selfish friend. But when you realize your friendship has been taken advantage of, you have full permission to put yourself first and stop giving more of yourself away to people who aren't giving you anything in return.

Boundaries are ways that you say no to people, sometimes without even having to actually say no. But saying no to a friend doesn't always have to be as harsh as it sounds. If you don't want to hang out in a big group because you're tired and need a night alone, it's okay to say so. If you've been giving a friend endless advice on her latest boy drama and you just don't have anything helpful left to say, it's okay to say so. Phrases like "I'm sorry, I really need to get my own stuff done today" go a long way in times like this.

Trust your intuition when you set these boundaries. Your gut feelings are your intuition, and they're also your guardian angels. Don't ignore them, but rather acknowledge their presence and be thankful for them. Intuition works hand in hand with logic, the true facts of a situation with your emotions removed. If you pretend to look at your life from the outside and someone you know looks like they're bad for you, let that logic team up with your intuition to figure out a solution that works for you. When you use your intuition and logic together, you'll always make choices that feel good to you.

Sometimes boundaries mean knowing which friends are good for which activities. Not every friend in your life is the kind of friend you can bare your entire soul to. Not every friend is someone you can be silly with on FaceTime for hours every night. If you're lucky, you'll get one or two ride-or-dies in your life you can do both with. For everyone else, it's okay to have different friends for your different needs. I know I'm not the friend people go to for a laugh, but my friends know they can come to me when they want to talk about the meaning of life. Being okay with that has helped me be a better friend to them, and it's made me grow my appreciation for myself and those friends too.

With practice, boundaries help you carve out space for yourself in your own life. The goal isn't to cut out your friends, but just to make sure you're living life on your own terms. And if friends don't take kindly to you needing space, hold firm to your boundaries. If they need to leech off of somebody, they'll find someone else who will let them. Sometimes people (including you) have to struggle alone until they figure out their own stuff.

I AM A RESCUER.

I will not allow anyone to be put down, including myself.

The path to being your authentic self is long, and it comes with setbacks. When we have friends who match our own levels of low self-esteem, for example, it might feel so good that you'll never want to change. Finally, you aren't alone—someone else feels the same way you do! And it's okay to share your insecurities with your friends, because that's what friends are for. But some people who know your weak spots feed on them and use them to make you feel worse. These aren't real friends at all—they're secretly bullies.

Recognizing secret bullies among your friends can be hard because they're so good at disguising themselves. One second, they may be mean. But the next, they may make up for it by inviting you to some exclusive group hang. Bullies know they're mean, so they keep giving you reasons to stay in their orbit. They need you so they have someone to control, and they like to take advantage of your kindness. They may cheat off of you on a test or have you help them shoplift, for example. They try to pay you back for helping them, but that doesn't change the fact that you still did something bad together. If you feel like someone is buying your friendship, they're manipulating you.

Or maybe whenever you see this friend, all they

do is say mean things about themselves or other girls. Of course, you want this friend to like you, so you say mean things about yourself and others to fit in. What you don't realize is that this friend is a bully, and you've started insulting yourself before your friend can—as if it hurts less that way. Except it doesn't. Being friends with bullies won't protect you from being bullied.

Bullies are also pros at gaslighting people. Gaslighting is a sly way of making you feel like you've imagined your problems, or that you're the one who is actually to blame in a situation where you did nothing wrong. When you confront someone about a mean thing they did, for example, they'll say, "What are you talking about? That never happened." Or, "Are you kidding me? That was your fault, not mine." If you've ever apologized to someone after they've hurt your feelings, you were being gaslit.

Bullies can also be really confused about what it means to be authentic. You'll find them walking around and saying mean things about everyone—to their faces or behind their backs—because they're just being "honest." And yeah, sometimes they can be funny about it! But people who fake honesty as an excuse for being mean aren't good people. Friends like this could turn on you at any second—and maybe they already have. Worst of all, you already know this, so you, too, find yourself being mean just to fit in. Friends who drag you down with them aren't really friends.

Whether someone brings out the best or worst in you is the difference between fitting in and belonging. *Fitting in* means trying to change who you are so people like you. *Belonging* means telling your friends, "This is who I am, and that's the only person I can be." No matter who you are, you deserve to belong—without having to be mean to do it.

Of course, friends really only become bullies if their behavior is consistently hurtful. If your friend has an occasional bad day and accidentally hurts your feelings, get curious instead of taking things personally. Ask them what's going on. Sometimes, someone else's behavior has nothing to do with you. You can only control yourself. Focus on the things you can control, and use logic and your intuition to figure out how to respond to someone else's bad mood.

Being the Bigger Person

It's important that you don't value your friends more than you value yourself. Friends are valuable, of course. But if your friends make you feel bad about yourself, or if you're embarrassed about how they treat other people, they're not your real friends. The same goes for your crushes, teachers, and coaches. Like we just discussed, loving yourself in spite of anyone who doesn't want you to is how you stay authentic.

You have two options for rescuing yourself from a friend who is secretly a bully:

1. Try to fix your friendship.
2. Stop being friends and move on.

No matter which option you choose, you have to have a conversation with your friend first. If you believe you're a good friend to her, be authentic to yourself and don't cut a friend out of your life without giving her a real chance. It's going to be hard, but it will be proof that you've been the bigger person all along.

Start by talking to your friend about what she's been doing that's been hurting your feelings, and how you've been hurting your own feelings too. Let this friend know about her good qualities—maybe she makes you laugh, is good in school, or has the best taste in music—and how much you wish she saw those good things in herself too. If she's been stuck in her own cycle of self-hate just like you, she probably hasn't had anyone try to make her feel good about herself like that before. Try making a pact for the two of you to actively start complimenting yourselves and other people more, to replace your habits of hate. This is the best-case scenario; you're repairing a toxic friendship and saving your friend alongside you.

But what if your friend doesn't want to be rescued? Sometimes, for reasons that aren't your fault, your friend may not be able to stop hating herself and others. If your encouragement toward positivity is received by her getting angry and lashing out at you in a hurtful way, that's a big sign that you have to move on. It means you're growing and your friend isn't—and maybe you've outgrown her.

If she agrees to try being more positive in the moment but just can't commit to it in the long term, sooner or later you're going to have to move on to better friends for you.

When I was growing up, I spent a lot of time with another girl at church who was really involved in the music department with me. She became the person I talked to about everything. For years, I thought we were close friends. What I didn't realize was that I was usually the only one talking in our conversations. She never told me anything about herself. One day, when she casually mentioned that she had a tattoo, I realized I didn't know her at all. I had no idea she had a tattoo!

It bothered me that she had let me get so close to her without her ever letting me into her life. Friendships are supposed to be balanced. I *wanted* to be someone she talked to about personal things. At first, I thought maybe the problem was me, that I just hadn't been asking her enough questions about herself. I tried to ask her more thoughtful questions, but she would always respond vaguely, never with the kind of depth you reserve for your closest friends.

Because changing my behavior didn't fix anything, I knew I wasn't the problem in this situation. So one day I confronted her about our one-sided friendship. I told her I cared about her a lot and I wanted us to be better friends. But in order to do that, I needed her to be more open and loyal to me. She agreed—she wanted that too—and said she would try harder at making me feel valued.

I gave her three more chances before I called it quits—and I wouldn't have been that generous if I hadn't truly loved her. The final straw was when my dad remarried. It was incredibly hard for me to see my family change that way, but she supported him more than she supported me. If she had truly been my friend, she would have told me it was okay to feel upset about his new marriage. When I finally cut her out of my life, it wasn't out of anger, but because I had accepted that she just wasn't who I needed in a friend.

It wasn't that she had been bullying me in this situation, but she wasn't being an authentic friend either. It feels like betrayal when you find out your friends don't value you the same way you value them. Back then, I was so desperate for a friend that I settled for less than what I deserved. Every girl deserves at least one friend who is as invested in their friendship as she is, and I wanted this friend to be that so badly.

Just know this: you can't fix someone, and it's not your responsibility to do so. No matter how hard you try, it will never work. The writer Maya Angelou once said that when people show you who they truly are, you have to believe them the first time. If you've done all you can to be honest with your friend and you still aren't being treated any better, it's time to rescue yourself and move on from that relationship.

When it comes down to it, your best friends are a reflection of who you are as a person. You deserve to feel good about yourself and to have people in your life who help make you feel that way. If you know you're a good person but aren't being treated like one by your friends—same goes for your family, crushes, teachers, and coaches—the problem isn't with you. The problem is with them, and you have the power to set boundaries and make it stop.

I AM A TRAILBLAZER.

I will use my friends as allies.

When Hillary Clinton ran for president in 2016, her campaign slogan was Stronger Together. It was a call to unite people of different political beliefs toward making real progress in this country, because it's hard to change things for the better when people blindly hate those they disagree with. We can also apply this message to our everyday lives.

You see, the world has a way of making girls hate each other. It feels like every day we're told we aren't good enough and that other girls are better than us. Whether they're people we know in real life or celebrities we see on Instagram, we start to feel threatened by them. Maybe you think one girl is a slut because she takes a lot of selfies, or another girl is a bitch because she has nicer clothes, or yet another girl is stuck-up because her grades are higher than yours. We hate ourselves, so we want to be someone else, but then we start to hate other girls for being who we wish we could be.

While we're spinning around in this endless cycle, we're too distracted by hating ourselves for what we don't have to instead love ourselves for what we do have. Think of all the things you could be doing with your time instead: running for student council president, practicing your favorite dance moves, or mastering a new sport. You could go swimming and truly enjoy it without worrying about how you look in a swimsuit. You could sing a solo in choir without being afraid of sharing your talents with the world. If even small things like these become hard when you hate yourself, it becomes so much harder to do even bigger things.

Girls are taught to second-guess and hate ourselves and each other to prevent us from setting big goals and actually achieving them, like becoming CEOs of huge companies, moving away from home to a prestigious college, or founding our own successful businesses. Self-hate prevents us from building confidence, the most essential thing we need to do these things we want to do. This cycle was created a long time ago by people who were afraid of what girls are really capable of, so they built a world that hides a very important truth. They knew what a lot of girls spend a lifetime trying to discover: when we love—instead of hate—ourselves and other girls, we become powerful beyond measure. We're strong on our own, but when we're together is when we become unstoppable.

It was historic that Clinton became the first woman presidential candidate ever endorsed by the Democrats or Republicans, but she wasn't the first ever woman to run for president. In 1972, Shirley Chisholm was both the first woman and the first Black person to run for president, even though she didn't receive the Democratic Party's nomination. If Chisholm hadn't run for president first, Clinton's odds might not have been as good as they were decades later.

Now, neither of these women ever won the presidency. No woman ever has—yet. But what they did do was slam a battering ram into a door that has been closed to women forever. Because these two women helped normalize what it looks like for women to run for a political office, we now have more women and people of color running other parts of the government than ever before.

Many people in this country feel threatened when they see a woman and/or a person of color coming at them with the power to change things for the better. They aren't used to what this new face of authority looks like. But what I'm telling you is this: *you* are what power and authority look like. The more girls who put on that face of power, the more normal it will become. All girls are powerful, and they're your allies and your fellow superheroes. Having your powerful friends by your side can remind you of your own power and make you feel a lot less afraid to do what you love and to make your world a better place.

Chapter Three
CARING FOR YOURSELF

Sometime over the past couple of years, it became trendy for us girls to take care of ourselves. You've probably seen it on Instagram. Maybe you've even posted pictures of yourself taking a bath with a glittery, colorful bath bomb; wearing a face mask that smells more like dessert than skincare; painting each of your fingernails a different color; or doing similar things. #Selfcare! But if you're doing these things just because they look good in your feed, are you really doing them to take care of yourself?

Basic hygiene is essential, yes, but it's not real self-care. Taking care of yourself means doing things that put you and your needs first, without performing them for an internet audience. That doesn't mean taking a bath can't help you feel better when you're feeling uptight and need some time to relax. In fact, that's a great time to take a bath. But it's just a Band-Aid on a situation that's really bothering you.

If you repeatedly feel uptight, for example, self-care means examining why you feel that way to begin with, then taking steps to change your feelings in the future. You have your internal junk and the junk that's going on outside of you in life, and that creates the perfect storm. Taking care of yourself means working on who you are. You may never be able to stop the stuff that bugs you the most, but you can learn to react to it less often. The temporary fixes you use to pamper yourself can help you fill in the gaps when you're feeling your worst, but don't forget to take the best of both worlds.

The goal of self-care is to protect one of the most valuable things you have: your mental health. Good mental health helps you get out of bed every morning. It helps you find loving friendships and relationships, and it helps you love others more too. Most importantly, it helps you love yourself. You are the one person you'll always be able to count on in life, and loving yourself will open more doors for you in life than anything or anyone else.

I AM FEARLESS.

I will love myself for who I am.

So how do you learn to love who you are? Believe me, it's hard to get it right the first time. You can't just flip a switch and start loving yourself overnight. It's something you have to remind yourself to do every time you feel pressure to be like someone you're not. Loving yourself means standing tall whenever you feel the pull to do something that feels inauthentic to who you are or that requires you to stifle a part of yourself for someone else's benefit.

If you're stuck in a cycle of inauthenticity, your real self starts to look a little scary. People often hide their real selves from their parents or friends, for example, because they don't want to be rejected by them. Nothing is scarier than not being loved, so you tuck yourself away in favor of who you think they want you to be, and you move further and further away from your true self. Loving yourself means breaking that cycle and embracing the things you love, the things that make you who you are, and the person you want to be. Loving yourself should feel natural, and that can be a scary feeling to adjust to if you aren't used to it.

An easy way to practice self-love is to find some time alone to get to know yourself and feel comfortable with who you are. Explore things you like and don't like, with no one else around to influence your opinion. What kinds of food, music, TV shows, and activities do you enjoy when you're by yourself? Compare that to the kinds of things you like only when you're around other people, and you realize how much of yourself was influenced by others instead of your own tastes and preferences. If you practice self-love in a small space, you'll gradually feel more comfortable sharing those parts of yourself with other people.

Writer and speaker Chip Conley created an equation: Authenticity = self-awareness × courage. When you build the courage and fearlessness it takes to get to know yourself, you're embracing your most authentic self. And my hope is that you'll learn to love her too.

Validating Yourself

Validation is the building block of self-love. This is the praise or rewards we get for a job well done.

Validation tells us we are good enough; we're appreciated for our actions and our selves.

There are two types of validation: external and internal. External validation comes from other people, like our parents and friends. It can also come from things such as being picked first to be on someone's team in gym, scoring high on a test, and other positive outcomes of your efforts. It feels good to see objective truths like these about ourselves: *I won the game, so I am good. My parents said I did a good job on my chores, so that means I am good too.*

It's dangerous to rely too much on external validation, though. Appreciating it when it happens is okay, but an essential part of loving yourself is knowing that your own positive view of yourself is more important than anyone else's opinion. That's internal validation. It's taking the external things that make you feel confident and moving them inward until you don't even need the external validation anymore.

Writer and speaker Scott Stabile sums it up well: "Let them judge you. Let them misunderstand you. Let them gossip about you. Their opinions aren't your problem. You stay kind, committed to love, and free in your authenticity. No matter what they do or say, don't you dare doubt your worth or the beauty of your truth. Just keep on shining like you do."

The external things that validate you aren't always dependable. Your parents might ground you. Your friends might betray you. You might bomb a test. These things hurt, but they don't mean you're a bad person. Find that little voice inside that says you're worthy of love, regardless of anyone else's opinion. Hold on to that voice, love that voice, and make that voice your own. It will make room for the rest of your self-love to grow.

I AM AUTHENTIC.

I will pay attention to what my body tells me.

At the beginning of this chapter, I talked about how true self-care isn't the same thing as basic hygiene. These things may help you feel better in the moment, but their effects are only temporary. They don't dig down deep inside you and fix the things that bother you on a recurring basis. Here's what true self-care looks like:

- Writing in your journal

- Taking time alone to sit with and process your feelings

- Going for a run or bike ride by yourself so you can think

- Seeking out support from trusted loved ones when you need it

- Going to therapy

- Taking medications if you have a diagnosed mental health disorder

These things help you get at the root of what's going on with you so that you can identify them, address them, fix them, and move on to live a happier life as your true self. We'll talk more about seeking out help, therapy, and medication later in this chapter. But first, let's learn how to identify what's bothering you—and that begins with listening to your body.

Here's an example: it's okay to be sad. But if you're sad every day, that's not normal. Watch out for whether that sadness turns into numbness, withdrawing or isolating yourself from your friends and family, and struggling to find joy in the things that used to make you happy. If you feel these things often and they don't go away over a long period of time, it could mean you're experiencing depression. Depression is very common and nothing to be ashamed of, but you don't have to accept that as your daily reality. You can fix it with therapy, and sometimes with prescribed medication.

Listening to your body is all about checking in with yourself regularly. Ask yourself if you feel happy, calm, and other positive emotions. If you start to stack up a bunch of no's day after day, that's a sign that you're not feeling like yourself, and you may need to seek help from a therapist. Being authentic is all about paying attention to how you feel, mentally and physically, so that you notice when things are good or when things are off and need to be fixed.

If you aren't sure what you're feeling emotionally, look for signs of how your emotions may be affecting other parts of your body. In children and younger people, anxiety commonly shows up as digestive issues. If you've ever gotten diarrhea before the first day of school, for example, that could have been your body's way of physically handling your anxiety so you didn't have to feel emotionally stressed.

When I was younger, I internalized my control issues so much that I was constipated a lot. I felt so little control over my life that I sought it out where I could—and since no one could control what was going on inside me, my body just held it in. Talk about an ineffective solution. I was eventually diagnosed with irritable bowel syndrome because this pattern became so ingrained in how my body functioned.

Whether your feelings show up physically or emotionally doesn't make a difference in the truth: something is bothering you. If you don't deal with it, it can come back to haunt you by developing into a bigger mental and/or physical health issue. That can stick with you for your whole life if you don't deal with the root of what's causing your problems. But if you seek out support and therapy, you can learn to cope with those issues in healthy ways and get back to living life the way it should be.

Unhealthy Coping Mechanisms

Bath bombs and face masks don't count as truly taking care of yourself, but there's one other ineffective coping mechanism we need to talk about. Healthy ways of coping with your feelings do *not* include vaping, smoking, drinking alcohol, and/or doing drugs.

These things may relax you temporarily, but they'll leave you worse off than you were before. The withdrawal effects of different classes of substances are often the opposite of what it feels like while they're in your system. For example, alcohol is a depressant, meaning it slows down your brain function and makes you feel more relaxed in the moment. But as your body naturally flushes alcohol out of your system, withdrawal effects kick in, stimulating your brain and making you feel anxious and overalert (not to mention nauseated and hungover).

Because your brain is still developing at this stage, these substances can also change your brain chemistry in the long run so that you can't function without them. This sets you up for developing an addiction—and that's not fixing a problem. That's just creating a brand-new one. If you're really looking to deal with your problems, you have to do the hard thing and confront them. The easiest way to do that is by reaching out for help from an adult you trust.

I AM A RESCUER.

I will take myself seriously.

Talking about mental health makes people feel so vulnerable. Girls especially want to be taken seriously, but we don't want to be viewed as a flight risk. So we often bottle up our problems and hide them from others. Sometimes we use humor to deflect how we're really feeling. If someone has ever texted you "How are you?" and you responded with something like "I'm depressed lol," you know what I'm talking about. That *lol* turns your sadness from something serious into a bad joke.

There's a double barrier around us whenever we're dealing with something hard. First, we have to believe what our bodies are saying when we notice that we don't feel good. Most of us aren't licensed doctors, so we have to convince someone else of the same thing in order for them to help us. And if we don't have someone we can trust who believes that our problems are real, it sends us right back to doubting that we have a problem in the first place—which makes it far, far harder for us to rescue ourselves.

In the Black community, mental health issues are often seen as weakness. And in the Christian community, they're seen as something that can be prayed away. These are the communities that raised me. So when I first started taking my anxiety and depression seriously, I had a lot of my own denial to work through. I couldn't believe I was the one going through problems with my mental health. It was hard for me to accept. Eventually I decided that I'd rather face it head-on and get the help I needed so I could become a better version of myself. That felt way more important than what anybody else thought or had to say. To this day, I'm still not sure my family believes I have something serious going on. But mental health is a very personal journey, and I continue mine because I want to be whole.

Fight that little voice inside that tells you to minimize your problems. Fight stigmas in your culture that tell you you're weak. Fight to have your voice heard if the people close to you don't believe what you have to say. You know yourself better than anyone, and you deserve to be taken seriously.

Going Through It

Here's the good news about therapy: anyone can benefit from working through their problems with a therapist, regardless of whether they have a mental health diagnosis. We've all had bad stuff happen to us in life, and it doesn't always turn into a diagnosable medical problem. Either way, you're always going to have to relive old stuff that happened to you, process it, and learn how to move forward. That's how you grow into a healthy person. Otherwise, a part of you will always be stuck at the age when that bad thing happened.

Seeking out therapy was the greatest thing I've ever done for myself. When I first went, I was nervous that it would reveal something really ugly about myself. Instead, I ended up learning a lot about my upbringing, my parents, and my role in my family's dynamics. I came out of that first session knowing more about who I was and who I wasn't. It gave me a sense of confidence that some things that had happened to me weren't my fault, and it made me feel validated and seen. It made me feel like I wasn't crazy after all.

Going to therapy is sometimes euphoric because you learn a lot not just about you, but about the other people in your life. But they aren't in therapy with you—you're the only one there, doing the work to better yourself. So in order for you to remain successful in therapy, you have to accept that you'll change, not the people around you. And if you can hold on to that, it will be easier for you to continue to grow.

I started therapy because I wanted to be better for my family, but then I realized I couldn't be better for them unless I was better for myself first. I'm still learning that. I don't think it's something you ever arrive at, but you become more aware of it as you grow. We evolve as people over time, but we never stop striving toward being our best selves.

Starting therapy was one thing, but starting medication was a whole other thing I had to accept. I'm somebody who is used to fixing everything for everyone else, but I couldn't ever fix anything for myself. When I found out that therapy alone wouldn't help me and I needed daily medication too, I felt defeated and powerless. I left like I didn't have any control over what was happening to me.

But I took the leap of faith and got the medication I needed anyway. Just like Tarzan swinging through the jungle, in order for the next vine to appear, sometimes you have to jump off the one you're on. I had been on my vine for a very long time—the vine of denial, of just getting by and trying to hold it all together. But I wasn't winning. I was losing myself. The tighter I tried to hold on to that vine, the more it was slipping away. I got to a point where I felt like I had nothing else to lose, so why not try medication and see if it helped?

My medication doesn't make me perfect. I don't think anyone ever really can be. But I'm doing a lot better than I was before I was on meds. Every day brings a new challenge, but the tools I learned through therapy and the medicine I take help me get through the things that are still painful.

Seeking Out Support

Let's say you've been listening to your body, and something doesn't feel right. You've accepted that, you believe it's real, and now you're ready to reach out for help. Good for you! Now what?

This part can be tricky. Like I mentioned earlier, sometimes the people in our lives don't believe us when we speak up for ourselves. While it's ideal to have the support of your parents when you seek out help for your mental health, that's not always the case. The good news is, even if no one in your immediate circle is able to support you, there are other people who are trained to help people just like you. All you have to do is find them.

Start at school. Check with your school counselor to see how they can help you. They can often refer you to someone else, depending on your needs. If you're unsure of who to reach out to at school, ask your favorite or most trusted teacher to connect you with someone who can help.

If you don't feel comfortable reaching out for help at school, some states allow people under the age of eighteen to seek out therapy without a parent's permission. Google "minor consent laws" to find out what your state's policy is regarding how old you must be in order to consent to mental health care on your own. If you qualify, try searching for reputable therapists in your area with websites such as Psychology Today or through an app such as Talkspace.

The help you need exists, even if it doesn't seem easy to obtain at first. But if you believe what your body is telling you and take those signs seriously, someone else who is trained to help people in your situation will be able to give you the support you need.

I wish everyone were better trained to talk about mental health issues. If that were the case, a lot of people would be struggling with them way less. Personally, I *have* to be open, vulnerable, and transparent about my mental health issues. Doing that disarms people and helps them open up themselves. At the very least, it helps them be honest about what's going on within them. And you never know who you're talking to. Maybe someone is struggling with suicidal thoughts, thinking about running away, or giving up on their medication and therapy. So I always show up as who I am—good, bad, ugly—and I hope it puts other people at ease.

My only rule for sharing your struggles is to make sure you feel safe around whoever you're talking to. Make sure you feel validated by them. Make sure that you don't feel like you have to explain yourself too much, or that you don't feel guilty after you talk about what you need and what you're feeling. Those gut reactions are the warning signs that this person isn't safe for you. Make sure that person is celebrating your authenticity, not just tolerating it.

A lot of people feel differently, though. They believe that others have to earn the right to hear your personal stories. Your honesty can be hard for these people to take, but I look at it as a breath of fresh air because there are so many fake people in this world who don't want to share or be vulnerable. They would rather pretend that all is well. They would rather look right than be right. I've played that game for most of my life, and for me, that life looks like death. So I always share my story from my heart, and that's what makes me stand out.

I don't always have the biggest support system in my life, so that's why I created the Real Girls FART mantra. I wanted to create something to help other people, and by doing so, it helps me. You can do that too. If you can't find what you need, create it. People will come to you, and they'll respond out of the authenticity of what you made because you built it out of your greatest need, not because it's cool or trendy. If you don't have a support group or system, start one. You don't have to wait around until it finds you first—everything you need to rescue yourself is already inside of you.

I AM A TRAILBLAZER.

I cannot control everything, but I can control how I treat myself.

By now, you've probably noticed that preserving your mental health is the central goal of taking care of yourself. All this is not only to help you right now, but also to make your life easier as it goes on. Working on yourself—and working through your issues—isn't about trying to change who you are right now. It's about becoming the best version of who you've been all along. It's about ensuring that you're happy, calm, and in love with your most authentic self.

It takes practice to get there, and you'll probably have to practice it your whole life. Most of us do. Once you get the hang of it, though, it can feel like a frustrating setback when you see other people in your life still expecting the same things from you as they did before. Remember that you've been the one in therapy, working on your personal growth—but others in your life are still stuck in their old ways. You have to accept that, but not without fighting to make space for yourself in your world.

Shame is one of the biggest obstacles you'll face while you're blazing your own trail. Shame is sneaky, and it's different from guilt. Guilt says, "I've done something wrong," and shame says, "I *am* wrong." Guilt is based on shoulds and rules that aren't your own. It comes from anxiety and the belief that you can only be happy if everyone else is happy. Shame and guilt are also cousins of fear—the same fear that keeps you from embracing your true self in case others don't like you.

The reality isn't that those people don't like you. It's just that they've been benefitting somehow from you being someone you're not. Think about the things you struggle with, the things you feel pressured or pulled into doing, the things that stress you out more than they help you. If you weren't secretly afraid that someone would get mad at you for not doing that anymore, you probably would have stopped by now, right? There's a way to fix that: you have to put yourself first.

Put Yourself First

Shame and fear drive our subconscious desires to overperform. When we try harder and harder to make other people happy, we tear ourselves apart in the process. After a while, it feels like these people depend on us. We're their shoulder to cry on, their homework helper, or their human security blanket.

As trapped as we feel by our unseen obligation to them, we also feel like we have power over them because they can't survive this way without us. And power feels good—so good that it's almost worth all this pain we're putting ourselves through to get it.

But putting yourself first also gives you power— the kind that doesn't hurt.

I've spent my whole life learning this lesson. Because I wasn't able to deal with stuff that happened to me in my childhood in a healthy way, little parts of me on an emotional level are stuck at that age. I was never able to work through those issues and grow those parts of me at a time when they were supposed to be growing, so I'm still working on them now. One of those issues always brings me back to when I was about twelve years old.

Back then, things in my family were rough. My parents fought a lot, and I not only witnessed it but also had to put them back together after the fact. Early on, I learned to be a protector in my family.

I lived my life to meet the needs of my parents. Because of this, I became especially close to my mom in a really unhealthy way. Sometimes I'd find her crying after she had a fight with my dad, and I'd be the one to wipe away her tears. My mom came to depend on me emotionally, and she told me all of the bad stuff that was going on between her and Dad—stuff that no child should have to know about their parents.

It can feel good when your parents tell you a secret. It makes you feel older, like you have their trust. But for me, it quickly turned into feeling like I was the parent in the situation, and my mom and my dad were little kids who fought all the time. A child should never have to feel like their own parent. I had my childhood taken from me because of the role I played in my family. Whenever I played with Barbie dolls as a kid, the scenarios I played out always ended with the Barbies getting a divorce or going to therapy. Even to this day, I still don't really know how to play games or be silly.

I was always there to comfort others when I was a kid, but no one was there to comfort me. Whenever I've tried to talk to my parents about the emotional baggage they've left me with, their responses always try to shame me for prioritizing my own feelings and for picking an issue with them. "How dare you?" they say. "You're going to miss me when I'm gone." I always leave these conversations apologizing for bringing it up in the first place, and I'm still working to stop reacting that way. All these years later, I'm learning how to reparent myself.

Girls are raised to feel ashamed anytime we put ourselves first. We're taught that it's our place in the world to take care of other people, not ourselves. That couldn't be further from the truth. Taking care of ourselves first and foremost is the main ingredient to living a life that makes us happy and that feels true to who we are.

Resist Overproductivity

We can talk a big game about taking care of ourselves, but sometimes it feels like we don't even have the time to do it. Life feels endlessly complicated. Maybe you take advanced classes in school or take part in several extracurricular activities—and that's on top of your responsibilities to your friends, family, and maybe even a job. And it feels like you have to balance all of it at the same time, because if you don't, you look like a slacker compared to everyone else.

Still, there's nothing wrong with slowing down your pace to catch your breath. Who cares what other people are doing? And who cares what they think about you? If you need a moment to pause, take it whenever you need it.

We live in a world that has confused overperforming with doing the bare minimum. This world has trained us to think we need to do the most we can at all times just to stay relevant. But once we get to the top of our game, there's nowhere else to go. This puts constant pressure on us to be perfect at school, at home, and elsewhere in life. Over time, that pressure can turn into anxiety, and that anxiety can turn into a permanent thing in your life.

Fight back against that pressure by setting boundaries with your time. Use those boundaries to carve out time in your schedule that's just for you and nothing else. Every day, spend a few minutes writing in your journal, lying on your floor and listening to music, or doing anything else that relaxes you and leaves your mind free to check in with yourself and see if you're feeling calm and happy.

Depending on what your future goals are, it doesn't always make sense to cut back on your workload in or out of school. But again, you have to keep checking in with yourself to make sure the burdens you are carrying are ones you—and only you—want for yourself.

Shame and guilt drive a lot of the pressure we feel to do things for others instead of ourselves. Here are some things you should never feel ashamed of or guilty about. What else would you add to this list?

- Not getting all As at school
- Not liking what everyone else likes
- Declining a call or not texting back immediately
- Saying no to things you don't want to do
- Standing up for yourself
- Doing what's best for you
- Doing nothing or being unproductive every once in a while

- Your imperfections
- Your body and your weight
- Mental illness
- Feeling sad

Crushing it in life looks way different for everyone, and it may not always show up in obvious ways—it's how it shows up over time. True success isn't based on productivity in one given moment. Everyone can sprint, but not everyone can go the distance and run a marathon. Will what you're putting yourself through today get you to where you need to go? Only you can answer that question. Only you can tell if the path you're going down is the one you want to be on.

Chapter Four

MENTAL HEALTH

In the last chapter, we talked about how taking care of ourselves means taking care of our mental health. Now, we're going to get even more real about mental health. Even though our world is gradually becoming more open about talking about mental health struggles, we still have a long way to go to make society more comfortable with talking about them.

I'm here to help you with these tough conversations, not to judge you for feeling one way or another. If this chapter feels overwhelming, the true realities of mental health may still feel foreign to you. My goal is to make you feel more comfortable talking about it so that it's easier for you to get help for your issues if you need to. You may have to come back to this chapter more than once in order for it to all sink in. No matter what, I want you to know that you're not alone. Other people are going through what you're going through—they survived it, and you will too.

I live with anxiety and depression. These are two very common mental health issues that people struggle with, but there are many others too. Check out the mental health guides at the back of the book to learn about other common mental health issues and how to deal with them in healthy ways.

Just because these things are common doesn't mean you have to accept them as normal—and they definitely won't leave you alone unless you deal with them. Going to therapy and (if your doctor thinks it will help you) taking medication are the most effective ways of dealing with these recurring issues.

Like I mentioned in chapter 3, depression is more than just feeling sad once in a while. Depression means feeling sad constantly, and withdrawing from all the people and things in your life that you used to enjoy. On the flip side, anxiety means more than feeling nervous before a big event. Anxiety is constantly worrying about what will happen next. It turns your brain into a hamster wheel of *what if, what if, what if?*

I like to describe anxiety as living too much in the future and depression as living too much in the past. But what about your life right now? If you don't deal with life, life will deal with you, so you have to struggle forward. Progress starts with confronting your issues and going to therapy. That may feel hard, but it's an investment in yourself and your future happiness. That difficulty goes away after you give it a couple tries. Things have to get worse before they get better.

I AM FEARLESS.

What I feel and experience is valid.

Depression, anxiety, and other mental health issues can be debilitating. That's why it's so frustrating that many people think these are choices instead of serious challenges to our health and well-being. I want to change how people perceive mental health issues because I want people in the future to be free from the judgment I faced. That way, people can focus on honest conversations about their health. I want to focus on the solution rather than the stigma. If I let other people's judgments decide whether I should take my mental health seriously, I wouldn't be in the good place I'm in now, and I certainly wouldn't have written this book.

Even when people don't experience judgment from their communities, it can still be hard for them to honestly address their mental health. People quickly become ashamed of their anxiety and depression, and it leaves them feeling like they're hiding a big secret about themselves. It makes them nervous to think about others discovering how they really feel, so they label their own feelings as unimportant.

When you don't take your emotions seriously, you let other things in your life distract you from your mental health. It's easy to put your mental health aside to focus on schoolwork, after-school activities, or friends and family. We may worry that if we stop to think about our mental health, we'll let down ourselves and the people who depend on us. That couldn't be further from the truth.

Your mental health isn't something you think about once you solve every other problem in your life. Good mental health is the foundation of a life where you're at peace with yourself and live free from damaging thoughts and feelings. Sadness, anger, and loneliness aren't damaging feelings by themselves. In fact, in a fearless journey to mental health, it's super important to acknowledge that we're complicated people with a wide range of emotions. It's okay to not be okay. No emotions you feel are so terrible that you need to hide them. Deep emotional pain is a part of the human experience, and it doesn't make you a bad person. There's no reason to feel ashamed of your uncomfortable feelings. They don't make you defective or unworthy; they just mean you're human.

Accept Your Feelings

In a moment of emotional pain, it can be hard to accept your feelings. The media shows us that happiness is almost the same thing as success, so feeling unhappy can make us feel like a failure. With any luck, our parents only want us to be happy, but sometimes they tell us that crying is a sign of weakness or that expressing our emotions is childish. But nobody on this planet has felt like a ray of sunshine every day of their whole life. No one is immune to emotions, so there's no reason for us to punish ourselves for feeling bad, as if that will trick us into feeling good all the time.

To have the strength to move through the hard times, we must acknowledge how we really feel. Once we aren't ashamed of feeling bad, we can recognize when we do feel bad instead of lying to ourselves and pretending we feel differently. Take some time to do the self-care activities we talked about in Chapter 3, then process how you feel. Remind yourself that it's not wrong to feel this way. You're not defined by your emotions—you won't feel this way forever. Giving yourself space to feel, even if it's uncomfortable at first, means you're more likely to heal.

Your hard emotions will eventually pass, but keep listening to your body to notice if they return. Notice how often those feelings come back to you and what may be happening in your life that triggers them. Notice whether other parts of your life may be affected by this pattern in your emotions and if it's making things consistently harder for you. Your emotions shouldn't feel like a burden—you deserve to feel calm and happy. When dark thoughts and feelings get in the way of your life, it's time to reach out for help from a therapist.

It can be hard to recognize the line between feeling sadness, anger, and nervousness and feeling a deeper, more serious pain. It can be a long, blurry transition between temporarily painful feelings to ones that interfere with your ability to function every day. That transition is especially blurry when you have to deal with upsetting life situations that you can't control, like trouble within your family.

Reach Out for Help

My anxiety started when I was young, but I didn't do anything about it—or even realize I had a problem—until many years later. Before that, I'd spent all that time hiding my feelings, even when I was bursting with them. If I'd known sooner that I had anxiety and there were healthy ways to deal with it, I could have saved myself years of unnecessary pain.

Whenever my feelings bring me to a dark place for a long period of time, I reflect on my early family life. My earliest memories are of the tension between my parents. My parents had been hurt by their own parents, and they took out their hurt on each other. Things between them could change from good to bad in an instant. This made me nervous because I could never predict what might happen between them. The one thing that was always constant was change, and all I craved was stability. I wanted a space where I could safely exhale. The problems in my parents' marriage made me worry about what I could and couldn't control, and that bled over into me wanting to control other parts of my life.

What I observed as a child also encouraged me to hide my feelings from the world, even when I needed help most. My parents hid their suffering from our congregation and their friends, so I learned that hiding hard emotions was the best way to deal with them. Now I know that I don't need to feel shame over my sadness or nervousness. In many ways, those feelings were reasonable reactions to the things I experienced.

Reflecting on my upbringing and my emotional health was a long process that I didn't start until I was much older. I only acknowledged my emotions when I reached a breaking point and knew that I couldn't hide them any longer. I planned my life around hiding the state of my mental health because I was ashamed. I didn't always ask for help when I needed it.

Now, fearlessly looking at my emotions and how they related to my experience growing up gives me insight, and that insight feels like control. Because I know how my mind works and the reasons why, I'm able to process my bad feelings and move past them much faster and easier than I would have otherwise.

I hope you never get to a point of emotional crisis in your life. I hope you'll be able to recognize the times when you feel terrible for weeks or months and reach out for help. I want you to know that you're not alone in your hard experiences, and that any difficult emotions you feel don't make you a bad person. Your bad emotions don't mean you have failed or that nobody will accept you.

I challenge you to look at your emotions as they really are, and not as you think they should be. I challenge you to accept what you're feeling, and then to explore what you're feeling. When we take an honest look at our situation, emotions and all, we can begin to heal and move forward.

I AM AUTHENTIC.

I reject the stigma.

I love the phrase "struggle forward." Struggling sounds like a bad thing, like we're being held back or fighting to keep our heads above water. Struggling forward, on the other hand, is continuing to make progress toward a better life even when you face obstacles. Although nobody should need to go through pain to gain new insights about their life, sometimes our struggles take us deep into our hearts and minds.

But it can be hard to see beyond the struggle. At first, I saw my diagnosis of anxiety and depression as a weakness. I thought that I, of all people, shouldn't have this problem. I'd grown up in church all my life, and mental health can be a taboo topic when you're Black and Christian. We don't talk about anxiety and depression as real illnesses. Well-meaning people would pray over me and say, "God, give her peace." They didn't have a clue what I was going through.

To me, their prayers felt like a dismissal of the problem. It was as if they wanted to acknowledge my pain, then tell me not to think about it again. I felt like they weren't taking it as seriously as other health problems like diabetes. When someone is a diabetic and has insulin issues, do we pray over them and ask God to help stabilize their blood sugar? No. Diabetics take medicine to help their body process certain foods, and they avoid other foods altogether.

Mental Health Equals Real Health

Mental health issues are also very much related to our physical health. Many mental illnesses are caused by a chemical imbalance in the brain. In my case, my brain doesn't produce enough serotonin or dopamine (the body's natural chemicals that help us feel at ease). Telling an anxious person to calm down or not to worry is like telling a diabetic person to eat some bread. It's a simplistic response to a complex problem.

With anxiety, the body physically doesn't know how to respond to stress. Maybe you've heard of fight-or-flight responses before. My brain and body can respond to my life like a fight-or-flight scenario and release too much adrenaline, which makes me feel completely drained afterward. There are times when I wake up and feel lousy before my day has even started. Those moments occur less often, but they still happen.

Sometimes my anxiety would morph into a full-blown panic attack. Panic attacks are an experience of complete fear and anxiety. Your heart pounds, your breathing becomes fast and uncontrollable, and you feel nauseous or sick to your stomach. It feels like you're trapped in a body you can't control. Other times, you may experience depersonalization, where you feel like you aren't connected to your body at all. Symptoms are different for different people, but all panic attacks have one thing in common: they're intense moments of emotional pain that's out of your control.

The stigma around mental health tells us that people only "perform" depression, anxiety, or other mental health issues for attention or acceptance. It also tells us that people who are struggling with mental health are somehow immature and unable to conduct themselves as adults. That's not true.

Part of rejecting the stigma around mental health means acknowledging mental health problems for what they really are: medical issues. It means having an honest discussion about the ways mental health negatively impacts different people every day. When we acknowledge the scope and reality of these issues, we'll be better able to direct people to resources that can help them heal. We can also look at the lifestyle and environmental factors that contribute to problems such as suicidal ideation, eating disorders, and panic attacks. Instead of dismissing them as weaknesses or ways to get attention, we can treat them as serious threats to the well-being of people in our communities who deserve support, peace of mind, and good health.

To put it simply, rejecting the stigma around mental health begins with understanding not just ourselves, but also other people. This is a movement to make your own life better as well as everyone else's lives. The stigma around all mental illnesses comes from our refusal to see them as they really are. We have stereotypes about what it looks like to be depressed, to self-harm, or to be anorexic. Those stereotypes aren't the reality of mental illnesses, which affect regular people every day.

Just as it's so important to be authentic to ourselves about how we feel, it's equally as important to respect and learn about what other people are going through. When we look past the stereotypes and learn about others' experiences without judgment, we help make it easier for those people to get the help they need and deserve. We can make them feel supported; and if we too are struggling with mental health, we can feel less alone.

I AM A RESCUER.

I will advocate for myself.

I know firsthand how crushing mental illness feels. When I'm going through a phase of high depression and anxiety, I can feel hopeless, as if I'll never get better. Yet when I meet other people who tell me about their own struggles with mental health, I don't see people who are hopeless. I see people who are strong and who deserve to overcome. I see people who will go on to have a positive impact in other people's lives when they share their stories. Even when their pain is most severe, I know there will be a day where it's no longer so crushing.

I also know hope can be hard to find when you're trying to deal with your mental illness alone. In my journey, many people have helped me. From my family to my friends to my therapist, I have people on my side to lead me through the tough times. But it wasn't always that way. I also remember a time when I was afraid to tell other people what I was going through. I thought they would judge me, or that they wouldn't take me seriously.

The day that my doctor diagnosed me with anxiety and depression was a turning point for me. When I walked into his office, I felt humiliated because I'd been crying and I hadn't slept. I felt like the people behind the desk at the clinic were judging me, and I was ashamed for showing such raw emotions in public. But when the doctor treated me with compassion and told me my diagnosis, I knew it was time to stop feeling ashamed. As much as I didn't want to ask for help, I realized I needed it.

What to Expect in Therapy

Let's say you've been doing everything right by taking care of yourself, listening to your body, and trying to work through your problems on your own, but something still doesn't feel right. Every day, you wake up and go to bed with this big, heavy emotional weight on your chest. Life like this is exhausting! When your mental health interferes with your ability to go through life as usual, it's probably time to see a doctor or a therapist. You don't deserve to feel bad for weeks or months on end.

When you see a therapist, they work with you to talk through those situations in your life that make you feel unworthy, depressed, nervous, or angry. They're trained to give you helpful coping mechanisms to approach your life and your emotions. A therapist can help you gain new insights into why you feel or act the way you do. They can also help you confront emotional wounds from abuse and other traumatic experiences. They're there to support you, and they're someone you can trust.

Therapy can help anyone, regardless of whether they have a full-blown mental health diagnosis. But if you do, your therapist will help you properly diagnose and treat it. Many mental illnesses, such as depression and anxiety, are caused by chemical imbalances in the brain. If this is you, certain therapists (called psychiatrists) can prescribe the right medication for your symptoms. Something as simple as a

daily antidepressant can be just the thing to improve
your mental health.

How to Talk about It

I know from experience that going to a doctor or
therapist can be difficult. I was an adult when I finally made it to the doctor, and even then I only
went after I was already in crisis mode. Don't wait
until you literally can't go to school or get up in the
morning before you ask for help. If you're suffering,
you deserve help—and you deserve help now.

In chapter 3, we talked about who to reach out
to when you need help. But how do you even start
that conversation? Lots of people have trouble ap-
proaching someone to talk about their mental illness
because they're scared to "bother" them with their
problems. If that sounds like you, think about how
you feel when a close friend opens up to you. Most
of the time, we feel touched that they trust us, and
we feel motivated to help. Trust that the people close
to you want the best for you and won't be turned off
by listening to your deepest thoughts and feelings.

Once you pick a person to talk to, set up a time to
speak to them privately. If it's a counselor or teacher,

they should be able to have a discreet conversation with you in their office or classroom. If it's a friend or family member, you could go to a place like your home or the park. Choose an environment where you feel comfortable and have a certain level of privacy. Meeting at a specific place and time will not only make you feel better about sharing, but will also be a cue to the other person that you want to have a serious heart-to-heart. When the location sets the tone for the meeting, there's less pressure on you to get the other person in the right mindset to hear what you're going to say.

During your conversation, try to be as specific as possible about what you're going through and how you're feeling. This will make it easier for the other person to understand your situation. For example, you can say things like, "I've felt sad every day for two weeks, even though nothing bad has happened to me." Describe how long you've felt the way you have, as well as the intensity of your emotions. This is where journaling your feelings comes in handy. Even if you don't show your journal to anyone else, it's recorded evidence of your feelings! You can also talk about how your mental health has interfered with your life, like your ability to connect with friends or do homework. Talk about the way your mental health has impacted how you feel about yourself and how your feelings have changed over time.

Giving another person the opportunity to understand your situation is also giving yourself a chance for them to help you. Sometimes we expect the people closest to us to know what's going on in our personal lives, but it doesn't always work that way. They can't always tell when we're in a crisis, especially if we constantly hide how we feel. Asking for the support you need is the best way to actually get it.

Being There for Others

Many times, the person we open up to becomes someone we can count on for years to come. What saved me were my good supportive relationships with other women who I knew I could trust. They were women who were older than me and able to give me new insights into my life when I needed them, because they had been through some of the same things that I'd been through.

We can help other people by being supportive

friends and good listeners. Maybe you aren't experiencing mental illness yourself, but you know someone who is. If one of your friends opens up to you about what they're going through, you have an opportunity to show them loving support.

A supportive friend understands that mental illness doesn't define you. It's only one layer of your life. It's important to make people feel like there's nothing wrong with them, especially if they're going through a hard time. Ask your friend questions about how they're feeling and why. Listen to them talk through their problems. While you can't fix their problems for them, talking things through together is often what they need to come to their own decisions. When you show someone you're there to listen and not judge them, they feel less alone.

If you learn that your friend is a danger to themselves or someone else, or if they've already acted on dangerous urges, it's important to tell a compassionate adult. You're not betraying your friend by letting a trusted adult know about dangerous situations. If someone tells you they're planning to kill themselves, or if you know about someone's anorexia or self-harming, it's far more important to make sure your friend gets help than it is to avoid an argument with them. Even if they're angry at you in the moment, telling someone else could save their life.

To be an advocate for ourselves and the people we care about, we need to be brave. We need to be able to open up and be vulnerable with other people so that everyone can get the help they deserve. When we tell the truth about our situations, seek out support, and approach mental health without judgment, we're already far ahead of the game. We've given ourselves and others hope—and in a battle with mental illness, hope can mean everything.

I AM A TRAILBLAZER.
I will break the cycle.

In this life, we're always going to need the support of other people to get through the tough times, whether or not we experience mental illness. Our emotions and inner lives are too rich and powerful to stay hidden. But although our emotions are complex and powerful, they don't have the power to run our lives. There are many things we can do, beyond reaching out to others, to help manage our emotions. Grappling with our dark thoughts and feelings in a healthy, effective way is one of life's bigger challenges, but there are many tools you can use to help.

In my journey with anxiety, one tool I've found useful is to make a list of the things I know to be true. I've learned that many things I worry about never actually happen. It's easy to let your mind run wild through all sorts of scenarios, each more emotional than the last. But a lot of anxiety can come not from a situation itself, but from our assumptions about it. If your friend didn't respond to a text, you may worry you did something to cause their silence. You may think that they hate you, or that they're ignoring you on purpose. In reality, they may not be in the same room as their phone.

Another way to help with anxiety is to think about what you can and can't control. I'm a perfectionist, so I always want things to be a certain way. A lot of my anxiety comes from my fear that something will go wrong. When we trick ourselves into thinking we have absolute control, we become a slave to our problems or struggles. Many things in life will never be perfect, and we have no power over them. Those are areas where we can relax a little bit and learn to let things go. You can't obsess about the things you can't control; you can only process them.

Recognizing Your Old Selves

Remember when I said in chapter 3 that if you don't deal with life, life will deal with you? Little parts of yourself become frozen in your past whenever you aren't able to deal with hard feelings or a traumatic situation. As a result, the unhealthy methods we used to get over that pain come back to haunt us later in life, becoming our default reaction to processing new or similar hurtful situations.

One time, I was at a football game with my family. My anxiety flares up in social settings, and that day it was really getting to me. I barely knew anybody there except for one woman I'd met before, and she gave me a half smile and then didn't talk to me. I started to worry that she wasn't talking to me because she didn't like me. Even though I tried to push my feelings down, I felt this horrible wave of rejection. My thoughts began to race, and I couldn't focus on the game.

As I sat there, I started boiling on the inside. I

started to have this inner monologue about how I wasn't the cool kid at the table, how I didn't have as much money as the other people we were with, and how I was so glad I wasn't in school anymore.

All these scenarios went through my head, giving life to a situation that wasn't true. Instead of ignoring my anxiety, what I had to do was think, *There she goes again. There's the little six-year-old girl on the playground who was forced to play by herself and was* rejected *by her peers.* Sometimes our emotional responses come from how we've felt in other similar scenarios, and recognizing this can help us get through the moment.

I had to keep comforting and soothing myself, both the little-girl version of myself who had been rejected and my adult self in the present moment. When I started to acknowledge that my younger self was in the room and very much still a part of me, I was able to confront the rejection.

I began to think about other possibilities and the facts of the situation. Nothing this woman had done was wrong. Maybe she wasn't talking to me because she was just getting settled. Or maybe she was tired or having social anxiety herself. I started to soften up a little more; and by the end of the game, I had a great conversation with her. We were able to connect, and I was able to overcome my anxiety.

Things aren't always as bad as they seem. Even though the moment made me feel like she didn't talk to me because there was something wrong with me, that turned out to not be the case. This was an example of my inner critic coming out to make me feel hard emotions that weren't necessary or based in reality.

People with mental health struggles often have strong inner critics: little voices that constantly tell us everything wrong about ourselves from what we say, wear, and do. It helps to pay attention to what your inner critic says and then ask yourself if you truly believe what it's saying. When we tell our inner critic to back off, we can treat ourselves with compassion and move forward.

Soothing Your Inner Critic

Deep down, I still have this inner critic. From time to time, it tries to resurface. We all criticize ourselves. It doesn't matter where the critic comes from: overly critical parents, a perfectionistic streak, or a fear of failure. In some ways, the inner critic is good because it allows us to keep working toward our goals and can help us become better people. But at some point, enough is enough. The inner critic can become dangerous and out of control. You may pick yourself apart until there's nothing left, and even then you could continue to feel like you're not enough.

If those cyclical worries and thoughts persist, and if you're too overwhelmed to check the facts or tell your inner critic to back down, a physical distraction can give you a break from your racing mind. It helps to do activities that are simple and repetitive, like coloring or going for a walk. Bringing your attention to your physical environment by forcing yourself to interact with the world around you can give you some space from your thoughts and allow you time to wind down. Even practicing mindfulness, where you pay special attention to your five senses and what's going on around you, can help you take a break from your thoughts and feelings. Going for a walk, doing yoga, or even listening to a mindfulness app are great ways to break a cycle of anxiety. Then you can come back to your feelings from a new angle later on.

Lots of problems in life seem small, like feeling rejected at a football game, but we know these issues usually run much deeper. For me, they ran even deeper than being a little girl who the other kids rejected on the playground. Growing up, a lot of my experiences of rejection came from feeling rejected by my father. Investigating the parts of your life that set the tone for your emotional responses leads to deeper healing; and for me, my father rejecting me was an important journey into my emotional past.

When I went to therapy with my dad, I told myself it was because I wanted to work through my issues with him so I could be a better parent. I also wanted to learn how to deal with him better. In therapy, I learned about my dad's own struggles with depression and anxiety. It made me have more empathy for him, and it made me realize there was a huge genetic component to my mental health issues. I also learned that I didn't have control over my dad, only my responses to the situation.

That was a huge weight off my chest, because it made me realize I could only own the issues that were truly mine to deal with. It helped me zero in on which issues I should spend time working on and which ones had nothing to do with me. I wasn't responsible for any of my dad's problems; I was only responsible for me.

Investigating deeper issues with your life can lead to new insights about yourself. It helps to keep a journal where you can think through your experiences and how they affect your day-to-day life. Writing often helps us think through the things that are bothering us instead of just feeling them. It can also be a way to give ourselves space and get to know ourselves better. Even the physical activity of writing words on a page can be soothing.

Self-soothing practices can show us the power we have over our thoughts and emotions, but there are definitely scenarios where they aren't enough by themselves. As always, it's important to recognize when our emotions become too difficult for us to handle on our own—and when we may need to see a doctor or a therapist to get the medical attention that we need.

What matters is learning to face our emotions instead of stuffing them deep down inside. In moments of reflection, it's hard to let shame make you feel more depressed. When we acknowledge our circumstances, we begin to see ourselves not as people who just can't "get it together," but as humans who are allowed to feel bad about the hard moments in our lives.

One of the most important lessons I learned during my journey to better mental health is to give myself space by crying when I need to cry and taking a nap even when I don't think I need one. I'm learning to pat myself on the back and say, "Good job," when I'm able to have hard, honest conversations. I can tell someone exactly how I'm feeling and make no apologies about it. I own what's mine, and I reject what's not. I know I deserve mental health and peace of mind, and I do everything in my power to keep those things by giving myself what I know I need.

Chapter Five

ROMANCE

et's be real. If you picked up this book for the first time, did you flip directly to this page? Romance is an exciting part of your life—you're finally ready to date! Maybe you've already gone out with someone at school. Or maybe you've been watching impatiently as your friends cycle through boy drama and you wait for your turn.

All we want is to feel worthy of love. But sometimes you may feel less worthy the longer you wait to find someone or if you've had a lot of relationships that always end. But that's not true! No matter what path you're taking toward real love, you deserve it; and it's out there in the world, waiting for you.

You don't need a guide to teach you how to love. When it's meant to be, it happens naturally and you'll figure it out along the way. Love itself is easy, but it comes with a lot of tricky obstacles to navigate. In this chapter, we'll talk about all sides of love, including not leaving yourself behind when you start a new relationship, having a plan in place for when breakups happen, and having control over your body when it comes to sex. When you've demystified all the grisly stuff no one talks about when it comes to relationships, you'll be even better prepared for some of the most fun and exciting years of your life.

I AM FEARLESS.

I will keep my heart open.

The best way to describe the feeling of having a new crush is *thrill*. It's part excitement about someone new and part fear about the worst that could happen: the other person not liking you back. In the first stages of a new crush or relationship, it's all about the butterflies in your stomach, the goosebumps on your arms, and the thrill in your heart about not knowing what comes next.

Part of that thrill comes from how unfamiliar and unpredictable your new crush is. But over time, you may see a pattern in who you're attracted to. In other words, you may find that you always go for the same type of person. Then one day, out of nowhere, you find yourself crushing on someone completely unlike anyone you've ever met before. That unfamiliar kind of love can be even more exciting and scary than anything you've experienced in the past.

Being vulnerable about your feelings with your crush means you're at risk of getting hurt. When you're young, it may feel like the only outcomes are that either they don't like you back or that you start dating and someday break up. Chasing your thrills and going after your crushes are important to learning more about yourself and what kind of love you want and deserve. Heartache is just part of the game. Ignoring it and going for what you want is what makes you fearless.

Dealing with Heartbreak

If you're doing it right, you'll likely encounter heartbreak more than once in your lifetime. The first person—probably even the first few people—you'll date is most likely not going to be your forever person, as much as that sucks to hear. It takes most people more than one relationship to figure out what kind of person they want to date. Rejection can look like a lot of things. Maybe your crush doesn't want to slow-dance with you at the school dance. Maybe someone doesn't want to go out with you. Or maybe your relationship ends with an ugly breakup. Sometimes you'll be the person rejecting or breaking up with someone else, which isn't always as simple as it sounds. No matter which side you're on, rejection never feels good, but it does get easier to deal with over time.

Eventually you start learning from these painful situations. For example, the end of an old relationship often comes with a chance to look back and figure out how to make sure the next person you date is an even better match for you. If someone hurts and rejects you before they even give you a chance, consider yourself lucky for skipping that mess—they didn't deserve you if they weren't willing to get to know you.

Because rejection is inevitable, approach it with a game plan. Figure out what makes you feel good when you're sad and hurt, and make time for those things when you need them. This could look like any of the following:

- Listening to sad music and writing in your journal

- Watching movies that make you laugh or make you feel less alone in your feelings (this is what rom-coms are for!)

- Indulging in a couple of yummy snacks

- Going for a run or spending time outside, taking in the fresh air

- Getting your nails done or buying a new outfit that makes you feel fierce

- Spending time around your best friends or family, who remind you of how much you are loved

There are lots of ways to make yourself feel better when you're sad. Figure out what helps you so that you know what to do if and when disaster strikes.

It sucks to be trapped with your bad feelings for too long, so it's important to have a cushion to land on when you're dealing with the ugly aftermath of a relationship or crush. Here, you can safely feel your feelings and deal with them in a healthy way. If you ignore them, you may end up agonizing over them in secret for too long.

I've always dealt with heartache by sitting in it at first and allowing myself to feel the pain of that situation. The more I try to escape the pain or rush through my feelings of grief, disappointment, and rejection or the process of ending a relationship, the harder it is to deal with overall. I learned early on that you have to cry it out.

One of my earliest memories of heartbreak happened when I was sixteen. A guy I had a crush on had been playing hard to get with me, which made me even more determined to make him like me. I saw him as a challenge, one I'd never found myself attracted to before. But it wasn't until I won and we started dating that I realized I was more attracted to the challenge than I was to him.

We dated for six months. Everything seemed fine in the beginning, but then I started getting this gut feeling that something was off. I couldn't figure out what it was. Then, one night, I had a dream that showed me he was messing around with another girl.

Even though it was just a dream, it matched the feeling in my stomach—and then other people at school told me my boyfriend was cheating on me. The girl went to a different school; and even though I'd never seen her before, she looked exactly like she did in my dream.

So I confronted my boyfriend. But it didn't go well at first. "What are you talking about? You're tripping," he said. I knew he was lying, and I felt like I was being gaslit.

A couple days later, he was finally honest with me over the phone. When he admitted to everything he had done, I broke down. I cried so hard that my nose bled, and then I passed out. I didn't know at the time that I had anxiety or that I was experiencing a panic attack.

Even though I broke up with my boyfriend because he had cheated on me, it still hurt. It felt horrible to be betrayed like that, and I learned from this relationship to hide my feelings and cut myself off from good relationships with people. In every relationship I had afterward, I always made sure I had the upper hand.

This kind of toughening up is one of the worst

ways to respond to heartbreak. I learned that the hard way. When you're in pain, you have to let yourself cry it out. Pain is part of growing, and growing is uncomfortable. It sucks, yes, but there's nothing we can do to avoid it. We all have to experience the things that make us who we are.

By responding to heartbreak by sitting in that pain, I let myself cry and take a nap when I need to. Yes, I'll watch Netflix for hours on end or call a friend to vent, but I never do that in place of allowing myself to feel that pain. We have to feel a little bit of that pain on our own—not all of it, but it's helpful to have time alone with it for clarity. Then you can start adding in other people.

Remember that if someone hurts you, they don't deserve you. Rejection or ending a relationship may hurt in the moment, but it's slowly pushing you toward something bigger and better that's truly worthy of you and all your glory.

Unfamiliar Love

Of course, when you finally find that bigger and better thing, it might freak you out. It's often a kind of love that doesn't feel like anything you've ever felt before. But in order to recognize it, you have to start by looking at your previous patterns of relationships.

We hate to admit it, but our parents influence the kind of love we seek. When we grow up being loved in the particular way our parents love us, that love is so familiar that we're often drawn to it in our romantic relationships. What have all your past crushes had in common? If they've all been funny, kind, or loud, think about who in your family may also express their love for you in similar ways.

But saying that the kind of love we seek out is predetermined by our parents is too easy. Yes, our parents love us, but some of us aren't lucky enough to receive the love from them that we really need. We find ourselves repeatedly dating people who are bad for us and ignoring people who have the kind of good, healthy love we deserve.

When I was sixteen, for example, I dated a guy who I was crazy about at first. But as time passed, things started going bad between us. He controlled everything about me, from how I talked to the things I did to the people I hung out with. He wanted to be the only guy in my life, and I had plenty of other guy friends who made him jealous. Bit by bit, my boyfriend was stealing my individuality by trying to govern everything I did.

If you're thinking this guy sounds like an overbearing parent, you're right. He was exactly like my dad. As the pastor of a church, my dad was very concerned about the image our family portrayed to the community. He controlled a lot about what I did because of that. He claimed he was just protecting me, but he was protecting his image too. Because of the way my dad raised me, I believed for a long time that love looked like someone controlling me in the name of protection.

I didn't date that boyfriend for too long, but it still took lots of time and therapy for me to figure out that I don't need someone else to protect me. The kind of love I was seeking because of how I was raised was toxic, and toxic love isn't real love. The real love I crave looks like freedom. It looks like someone accepting me for who I am, rather than someone who is trying to change me.

If this sounds like the love you want but aren't receiving from your relationships, you may have been raised on the wrong kind of love too. But it doesn't always have to be this way. When you find yourself falling for someone, ask yourself, "Does this person make me feel free? Does this person make me feel accepted?"

It takes a lot of work to begin trusting healthy love when it's unfamiliar to you. When we do finally meet someone who is good for us, it may not feel as exciting as the bad kind of love. Maybe it's boring, or it's scary enough that we run away from it. Sometimes it takes daily reminders (and therapy) to reframe how we think about what love is.

Never settle on dating someone who treats you poorly because you're afraid you don't deserve any better. You always, always deserve better.

Be fearless in the face of rejection. Be fearless in the face of love. The love of freedom and acceptance you're looking for is out there in the world, and it belongs to you.

I AM AUTHENTIC.

I will not forget who I am in a relationship.

Maybe this sounds familiar: you just got your first boyfriend, and you couldn't be more excited. Finally, someone likes you back! Nothing in the world feels as good as that, so you spend all your free time with him. You're obsessed with each other, and you don't care. Wherever he goes, you go too—and you start seeing less of your friends. You mainly hang out with him and his friends now, even though it makes you uncomfortable to be the only girl there. He even comes along to hang out with you and your own friends, and they get frustrated that they never get to see you alone anymore. You're so focused on your boyfriend that nothing else matters anymore, and slowly you become more and more isolated from your friends.

If this hasn't happened to you, maybe you've seen it happen to your friends. Regardless, the pattern is always the same. As girls, we're taught that our role in a relationship is only to please a man. Even if you aren't attracted to boys, you've likely been raised to feel some sort of obligation toward them. The paradigm of a male/female relationship has been gradually shifting toward equality in recent decades, thanks to brave women refusing to settle for less than the equality they deserve. But that doesn't erase the fact that, for centuries, women have been expected to shrink themselves in their relationships to make room for their boyfriends and husbands.

Shrinking ourselves for a boy can happen without us even noticing it. That's what happened to me when I was sixteen and dating the boyfriend who controlled me and my individuality. When we start going out with someone we really like—whether it's our first relationship or not—we can get so excited about the newness of someone liking us back that we don't notice that we're neglecting other parts of our lives. We get so boy crazy that we forget about our friends, our homework, and our own selves.

Forgetting who you are in a new relationship can be a lot more complex than seeing your friends less frequently. This stuff can happen before your relationship even starts if you feel pressured to change who you are to get someone to like you. Shrinking yourself starts on the outside, but it creeps inward and becomes increasingly dangerous to your authentic self. Maybe you started dressing differently to catch your crush's eye and completely changed your style to match theirs. Then you started getting into your crush's favorite music and movies, and talking and acting differently around them too. But all this stuff isn't authentic to you.

The shrinking doesn't stop until it affects your values—and nothing is more valuable than yourself. If you start making excuses for your boyfriend or crush treating you badly (whether they bail on you or always show up late, or if they hurt you verbally or physically), you're no longer holding any space of your own in your relationship. You've shrunk as far as you can go.

In the worst cases like this, it's clear you're suffering from that toxic kind of love we talked about earlier, rather than the freeing and accepting kind of love. When you're loved for being someone you aren't, the real you isn't being loved at all. We'll talk about setting physical boundaries within relationships in a moment. But for now, know that when you're searching for a new relationship, it's important to set a personal boundary so you don't change who you are to get someone to like you.

We feel a lot of pressure to devote ourselves to the people we date. We're rarely taught how to balance that with devoting time to ourselves or the friends we love as well. Your friends are more likely to accept you for who you are and stick around with you over time. Sometimes the love you need has been with you all along, and you don't have to chase down a crush for a synthetic version of it.

A new relationship should make you feel like your life is expanding, not shrinking. When you gain a person in your life, you shouldn't have to lose friends and your sense of self. No matter who you're dating, there's always room for you in your relationship.

I AM A RESCUER.

I will not let other people manipulate me.

The flip side to staying true to yourself in a relationship is not letting yourself be manipulated by the person you're dating. Manipulation is when someone tries to control what you do only for their own benefit, like when my boyfriend was trying to change me when I was sixteen. He had his own unhealthy reasons for wanting to be the only guy in my life, and I didn't stand to benefit from any of his other demands for me, like talking or acting differently. Relationships require compromise, sure, but both people should always benefit from it.

Manipulation has many different faces. Sometimes it looks like someone saying, "If you really love me, you'll do this thing for me." But master manipulators know how to do it without saying anything. All they need to do is make a pouty face, ice you out, and/or stop talking to you if you do something they don't like. You hate being treated that way, so of course you give them what they want to make them stop being angry at you. Remember when we talked about how friends can be secret bullies? Boyfriends can be secret bullies too.

If the person you're dating often makes you feel bad so that you'll give them what they want, think about whether you're really benefiting from this relationship. Being loved and cared for *only if* your person gets what they want from you first is another kind of unhealthy love. When you find yourself in this kind of situation, it's time to rescue yourself and break it off.

When you really love someone, putting yourself first can feel selfish. You know someone is mistreating you because they have their own troubles that aren't about you, so you worry you may be betraying them by distancing yourself or cutting them out of your life. But doing this doesn't make you a bad person, especially if your relationship has become toxic, abusive, or threatening to your safety.

Supporting Your People

When we talk about being a rescuer with your people, it's not about changing who they are because you don't like parts of them. You can never really change someone—they'll always be who they are. Rescuing your relationships (whether that's with your friends or your boyfriends) is about exchanging the kind of love that makes you all feel supported, accepted, and free. You are each other's safety net. You can't always prevent your people from getting hurt, but you can be there to help them when things go wrong.

So while you can't change your crushes or friends, you can try to bring out the best in them. Dealing with people who are secret bullies requires a different kind of love and patience. But if your people don't require tough love or extra help in being their best selves, you may find yourself with more room for having fun.

The rules of supporting your people are almost exactly the same whether you're dating or best friends. It looks like this:

- Giving each other compliments or regular affirmations of things you like about each other or things you're good at

- Showing up at their big events, like sports games or theater performances

- Not bailing on plans

- Listening to them when they're having a hard time

- Offering help or hugs whenever they need it

- Exploring new hobbies and interests together

- Always being honest, but speaking your truth from a place of love

Every relationship in your life, whether romantic or not, requires balance. We'll talk more about setting boundaries in a little bit. But right now, know that you should never feel like you're exhausting yourself by supporting your people. If you do, something is out of balance, and you may not be getting back as much as you're giving. Relationships and friendships are meant to be fun, not draining. They require equal amounts of love and attention from both sides. You have the power and the right to decide when it's not worth it anymore and you're ready to seek out a relationship that's less uneven, chaotic, and consuming.

I AM A TRAILBLAZER.

I control my boundaries.

When it comes to sex, it feels like there's no way for girls to win. We're sluts if we have sex and prudes if we don't. These concepts were created a long time ago by men so they could control girls and women by telling us what to do with our bodies. If you've ever felt ashamed about your body, you'll know what I mean when it comes to owning your sexuality too. The shame of being labeled a slut or prude has made sex shameful to talk about by association.

Making important topics like sex taboo, especially among young people, allows false facts and pressure to build up around these things we don't clearly understand. The reality is, sex is a lot less complicated and scary than the world will have you believe. But that doesn't mean it isn't something to take seriously.

Taking Back Control

The world is filled with people giving advice to girls about what to do with their bodies. Sometimes this advice looks a lot like that control I mentioned—especially when it comes to having sex. People describe having sex for the first time as "losing" your virginity, but I've never seen it that way. When you have sex, you shouldn't be losing anything, and it better not be stolen from you either. I prefer to call it "giving" your virginity.

If you think of virginity as something you *lose*, you may come away from your first experience with sex feeling empty. The language of "losing" virginity makes it sound like something you can't control, which may also lead you to have sex with someone you don't want to and then regretting it. If you *give* your virginity instead, you have full control over the situation. You get to choose who is worthy of that first experience with you, and you have the power to make it as special as you want it to be.

That being said, the concept of virginity only has meaning to you if you let it. Not everyone finds meaning in virginity. For example, sex has historically been talked about as involving a penis and vagina, but you may not be attracted to people who have penises. If you're a girl who is attracted to other girls, your first time having sex is still meaningful if you want it to be, regardless of whether you value the concept of virginity. No matter what people expect you to do with your body, you're the one who gets to decide how to label your experiences.

I was fourteen when I had sex for the first time. A lot of people had been telling me it was too early, and that sex was forbidden until I was older and married. The strong taboo around sex made me even more curious about it. So, to find out what it was all about, I had sex with the guy I was dating at the time.

I wasn't afraid to have sex. I had spent a lot of time thinking about it beforehand, and I was sure I was ready for it. I just wanted to know what it was all about. These two things—fearlessness and forethought—are essential to having sex for the first time. People say you should be in love with the person you first have sex with. That wasn't true for me, but I don't regret it. Giving my virginity to him wasn't something I did only for his benefit. It was something I wanted to do for myself, and I had complete control over the situation.

When we're taught that sex is forbidden, it makes us ashamed of our interest in it. If sex hadn't been presented to me as the ultimate taboo for a fourteen-year-old, maybe I wouldn't have wanted to have sex that early. Having more open and honest conversations about sex is key to reducing the intense pressure we feel around it from a very young age. Research shows that waiting to have sex later in life leads to better outcomes, like less risk of pregnancy and more overall satisfaction with the sex itself.

To be clear, I don't support teenagers having sex. It's okay to be curious and to openly talk about sex, but that's to lessen the pressure you feel to have sex earlier than you want to. Sex isn't as intimidating as it seems, but it's something to do with careful thought. The right time is different for everyone, and your time will come when you're mature enough to feel safe and in control of it.

Staying Safe

No conversation about sex is complete without talking about protection. Sometimes it's embarrassing to talk about. But when you really think about it, with all the value and pressure we put on sex in our culture, there's no reason to be ashamed of wanting to have safe sex!

Everyone—regardless of the gender of the person you're having sex with—needs protection during sex to prevent sharing sexually transmitted infections (STIs), such as chlamydia, herpes, gonorrhea, and HIV. If you're having sex with someone who has the opposite sex organs as you, you also need protection against getting pregnant. There's no benefit to ever catching an STI, so it makes sense to carefully avoid contracting one. Similarly, you may want a baby someday, but there are more challenges than rewards if you have one while you're still in school and charging your way through these years of life that are meant to be focused on yourself.

Girls and boys are both taught about the importance of contraception—mainly condoms, but also various types of medical birth control for girls, like birth control pills and the increasingly popular IUD. But the reality is that the burden of being protected falls on girls more than boys in sexual situations. Guys don't have to worry about getting pregnant, so they're less likely to think of carrying around condoms. Even though the person you're having sex with should also come prepared to avoid pregnancy and STIs, it's important to keep yourself prepared if you're sexually active so that you can always expect to have stress-free fun.

Contraceptive methods are protection against the consequences of sex that make it less enjoyable. Just as much as you need these physical forms of protection, you also deserve to be emotionally protected during sex. That kind of emotional protection is called consent.

Consent, Consent, Consent

You aren't the only person who needs to be in control of the situation when you're having sex or being intimate with someone. The other person needs to be in control too, and at an equal level as you. This is called consent. Historically, guys haven't been taught to value consent, so girls have learned to deal with this by protecting ourselves with pepper spray, a couple of self-defense moves, or being ready to scream if we ever get attacked while we're alone on a dark street at night.

It's a myth that you're more likely to be sexually attacked by a stranger. Sexual assault and rape are unfortunately far more common with someone you know. This person can use their familiarity with you to pressure you into doing what they want, even if it's against your will. Whether you physically and/or verbally protest or freeze up in panic because you're too afraid to stop it, this is sexual assault.

Consent used to be defined as "no means no," but a more progressive definition is "yes means yes." Someone can't be certain that you're consenting to be intimate with them unless you seem enthusiastic about it and are saying yes to the experience. If someone is saying no, their intentions are clear—it should stop. But if someone isn't saying anything, it's likely because they're too afraid for their safety to protest. They're ignoring their brain's fight-or-flight response and mentally playing dead until the experience is over. If you ever feel like you're mentally playing dead during a sexual encounter with someone, you haven't given that person your consent.

You should always be in equal control of every one of your sexual experiences. You can't be in control if the other person doesn't have your consent. Whether you consent because you're simply curious or because you're in love with someone, there's no "right" reason or time or situation to have sex. Simply wanting to have sex—free of fear or pressure—is the only reason you need to have sex.

Just as easily as you can give consent, you also have the right to take it away. If you're having sex with your boyfriend, for example, you'll eventually get to a point where consent is assumed based on your past experiences together. But if he does something that makes you not want to have sex with him, it's your right to say so. A guy isn't entitled to have sex with you just because you've had sex before.

If you aren't sure how to make the first move or if the other person even wants you to, just ask! Even if it's as simple as, "Can I kiss you?" When you've already started being intimate with someone, there's one easy question you can ask to make sure you have their consent: "Is this okay?" Teach this question to whoever you're intimate with so that they always know when they have your consent. It may sound dorky right now, but in the moment it's sexy for someone to care about how you feel.

Chapter Six

RESPONSIBILITY

Anything fun in your life has probably come with rules attached to it. Time limits on your first computer or cell phone, chores for your pet, a nightly curfew—these are all small ways your parents may have started introducing you to responsibility.

Sometimes we like having responsibilities. Other times, they're annoying. But we have to do them anyway because they make more fun things possible in the future. Being home by 9:30 p.m. on Friday night may not sound fun, but if you stay out past your curfew and get grounded from going out on the weekends for a whole month, that curfew starts to look pretty good compared to the alternative.

Responsibility is when we commit to doing things that change our lives for the better—not by doing something we care about once, but by doing it again and again. When we take responsibility, we OWN our lives and guide their direction in a way we want. Responsibility means that we understand what we can change about our lives, and that we take action every day to build a life we're proud of. Having responsibility means understanding what qualities we want to grow in ourselves and taking concrete action to grow those qualities.

Doing things over and over to meet a goal means we have to think in the long term. There will be days when we simply don't want to take care of our responsibilities. But part of the reason it's so important to do them anyway is that our responsibilities don't just change our lives for the better. They also benefit others. Whether you're involved in a group sport, a class project, or small jobs around the house, other people depend on you.

Even when we have to do things that we don't want to, we know that committing to our responsibilities makes our relationships with other people better. Everything changes when people know they can depend on you. Your family may be more likely to trust you at home alone, let you stay out with friends later, or pay for an activity you've always wanted to do. Your friends will be more likely to help you on any project you need help with, or confide in you because they know you're trustworthy. If you accidentally turn in your homework late, your teachers may be more forgiving because they know that's not like you. Life is easier when everyone is on your side, and showing that you're responsible helps convince them of this.

But responsibility is work, and sometimes you don't know how many responsibilities you should take on at a time. Having people rely on you can make you feel anxious. That's the hard thing about responsibility: as soon as you admit that you can take control, it can also feel like admitting there are things you don't have a lot of control over, like your grades or a friendship that's drifting apart. Yet even having the responsibility to admit our mistakes can make us more mature. Admitting our mistakes or identifying areas where we've dropped the ball can strengthen our relationships by proving we're honest people who want to do better. In the end, taking responsibility means being a person who is capable, motivated, and fearless.

I AM FEARLESS.

I will take responsibility for my actions.

You have the power to change your life through your actions. Don't let anybody make you feel powerless or like you don't have choices. The commitments you make to yourself and to others can help you create a life full of everything you love. Through your responsibilities, you can gain skills and relationships you didn't have before. You can also gain confidence by proving to yourself over and over again that you can do anything you put your mind to.

Put In the Work

A lot of people learn responsibility by having a job. During my second year in college, when I was studying public relations, the fire turned up underneath me. I was nineteen and working two jobs in addition to being a full-time student. One job involved me working part-time as a customer service representative for a credit card company—a normal, easy job for a college student looking to make some extra money. My other job was a different beast entirely: I was the leader of the music department at my dad's church.

That department was HUGE. I had to coordinate the band, choir, vocal ensemble, soloists, and all the special music for every service. I had to approve everything they did, attend every rehearsal, and show up to every service an hour or two early to prepare things. Did I mention that everyone I worked with was my parents' age? Some adults don't take kindly to a nineteen-year-old telling them what to do. So this job was hard and sometimes awkward.

I spent so much time running around for the job at my dad's church that I barely had any time to enjoy the fun parts about being in college. All of the friends, parties, and freedom—I missed out on that. But as much as I resented this job for the burden of its responsibilities, I reaped so many rewards from it.

The department came to me in disarray, because so many other people had left before me. So I had to rebuild the department from the ground up. I didn't know how to do this job when I got it, but I learned how to do it—and I did it well. It was a challenge, but it taught me how to be resourceful.

I knew I was doing a good job because once I

took over the department, more people started showing up to church. Our music inspired and uplifted everyone when they came to service, and they showed up on time so they wouldn't miss it. Soon, other churches in the area were requesting that our department help improve their music departments too. While I'd been so focused on the difficult daily tasks of my job, I had created a name for myself in the community.

Things got even harder in my junior and senior years, when I had to get an internship. I was still running the music department, working at the credit card company, and studying full-time at school. I used my coordination skills from my job at church to get an internship at the *Santa Maria*, the ship Christopher Columbus sailed on for his first expedition to the Americas. There, I wrote press releases and coordinated all the tours of the boat.

Even though I took on the responsibility of working multiple jobs much earlier in life than I wanted to, I became a better person because of it. I learned how to thrive in any situation, multitask and prioritize, and shine when things get dark. I stayed at my job in the music department until I was twenty-three, but setting the bar high for myself that early led to many greater opportunities for me later in life.

Own Up to It

You have the power to change your life, but when things get in your way, it can be hard to believe in your power. The media and people around us send us messages that tell us we don't matter. Those messages can take the form of a super-controlling parent, a friend who talks over us all the time, or a teacher who shoots down our ideas. Those experiences can make us feel limited in how much control we really have over our lives.

It's important to remember that when people do things that hurt you, it's not because of you. It's because of what's going on in *their* heads. Some people need to put others down to feel like they're in control. Just because some people treat you poorly doesn't mean you don't have power.

Television, ads, and movies often make you feel like it's "normal" to be something you're not so that you feel pressured to buy into their products and ideas just so you can feel normal too. Just because they have one idea of what's "normal" doesn't mean you're defective or powerless. It's up to you to believe in your power and worth.

When you don't believe in your own power, other people can take it away from you. You start to not care about anything, because when you don't think you have power, caring seems painful. Why care if nothing is going to change? When you believe you can't change things, you let others make your decisions, or you follow along with a group of people even if you don't agree with what they do. Yet even in the most difficult situations, we can change our own lives for the better, even if it's a small change.

Keep Your Values

Just because you feel in the moment that your actions don't matter doesn't change the fact that they do. When you don't follow your values, people—especially yourself—can get hurt in the process.

Ninth grade was the first (and only) year I went to a public school. Growing up in a Christian school, I was so excited for what public school meant for my freedom and my social life. Finally I had the chance to shake off my goody-two-shoes reputation and be a different person! I could become someone cool and well-liked who would get invited to parties. I could become someone who fit in. And I did become that person—but that version of me wasn't responsible enough to handle it.

Part of what led my transformation that year was a friend of mine at school. She had a bad reputation. She was promiscuous and made reckless decisions with her body. I didn't do any of the same stuff she did, but I exposed myself to it. So her reputation started rubbing off on me. I didn't like what she—and by association, I—was known for, but it was better than being an outcast. I'd always struggled with being different, and I just wanted to fit in.

As my reputation slipped, my sense of responsibility went with it. I behaved so badly that year, and I lied to my parents—a lot. My parents were most bothered by how boy crazy I had become. I was a serial dater. Even though I didn't have too many serious boyfriends, all my parents saw when they looked at me was someone too focused on having fun with boys to care about school, like I used to.

One day, toward the end of the school year, I had a big algebra test coming up. Instead of taking the test, my friend said we should skip and go to Dairy

Queen. I knew it was wrong to skip, and I wasn't comfortable with it. But I was still so desperate to be accepted by someone else. Besides, I had a C in the class, so I didn't think I'd fail if I missed the test.

As soon as we walked into the parking lot, my mom pulled up out of nowhere in her car. It was like she had read my mind. "What are you doing?" she said, angry and disappointed. I lied and said that school was done for the day. She didn't believe me. She made me get into the car and go home with her. She knew for sure that I'd lied once my report card arrived a couple weeks later and it said I had skipped the exam. Not only that, but I'd failed the class altogether.

I could have passed that class if I had at least attempted to take the test. I might not have gotten an A in the class, but I definitely wouldn't have gotten an F. Instead, because I gave in to the pressure and opportunity to be someone other than myself, I'd failed. My parents grounded me, then re-enrolled me in Christian school the next school year.

Once I was back in Christian school, my bad behavior stopped. Everyone knew who I was, so I didn't need to pretend to be someone else. The thing is, I could have been my true self at the public school, and then I probably would have been able to stay there for the rest of high school. Just because you change environments doesn't mean you have to change who you are as a person.

We should always aim to be true to our values. But for those times we slip up, we need to forgive ourselves and start over again. It happens to everyone, and it doesn't mean we're weak or bad. It only means we can do better.

Staying true to values and responsibilities is something many people—even adults—struggle with. Maybe you can think of a time when someone didn't keep their commitment to you, like a parent who didn't pick you up when they said they were going to, or a friend who flaked on you at the last second.

People usually don't intend to hurt you with their irresponsibility, just like you don't usually have bad intentions when you drop the ball on your commitments. Building awareness of the times we don't come through on our responsibilities is the first step to make sure we don't let others or ourselves down. We need to be fearless and honest with ourselves about what we can control and when we've made mistakes. Our actions have power, and we want that to do work *for* us, not *against* us.

It all starts with committing to something you care about and doing that thing over and over again until you learn more about it and get better. Lots of people are afraid of even starting to do what they want because they're worried they won't be any good at it. But being good at something isn't the point. That will come later. The point is to let yourself explore, to eventually pick an interest that you truly connect with, and to create a life that satisfies you because you're doing something you value. When you follow that passion with commitment, you're fearless in the face of failure. You do something even when it's hard, and you improve throughout the process. You feel like you're living a life of purpose because you took control of your future.

Believing in your power over your life and sticking to your commitments will not only help you create the life you want to live. It will also make you a kinder, more confident person. Struggling through the setbacks to master your passion will give you more empathy for other people going through their own setbacks. You'll care more about having a positive impact on others because you'll know firsthand what it's like to struggle despite all the odds. You'll have chosen the values you want to live by and be able to bring those values into all your relationships.

Defining your values is a very helpful way to zero in on your passion. Knowing your passion helps you know what specific responsibilities to take on to achieve a life you love. After all, you can always take on a lot of responsibilities that don't make you feel good about yourself and don't lead you to the life you want.

Think of responsibilities as building blocks. You can either use them to build the skyscraper of your dreams, or they can pile up into a prison. As long as you believe in your control over your life, you are the architect. Build what speaks to you.

I AM AUTHENTIC.
**I will make choices that allow
me to be true to myself.**

Responsibilities seem to accumulate as you get older.

At home, your parents may give you more work around the house or trust you to look after a younger sibling. There's more homework in school and more pressure to join extracurriculars and accelerated classes. Getting older also means you're becoming more aware of global problems like inequality and climate change. You're starting to notice more responsibilities to yourself, your family, your community, and to the world at large.

Responsibility can create a ton of pressure when there are high expectations for what we should achieve. Sometimes it feels like all the responsibility other people give us is crushing. Instead of allowing us to move toward a life we want and the person we want to become, it feels stifling. Responsibility is work, whether it's in our favor or against us; and when we don't feel like it's helping us become who we are, we can start to crack under all the pressure.

Growing up, I felt a lot of pressure to behave well because my father was the pastor at our church. My parents trained me to set a good example for the other children. While everybody saw me as some sort of golden child, people didn't realize I wasn't allowed to behave like the other kids. I wasn't able to play outside after church or be silly. Most days, I felt awkward. I stayed quiet because I was afraid that anything I said or did would embarrass my father or my family.

Back then, my responsibility toward my family overwhelmed me. I wished I had more time to be myself—or someone other than who they wanted me to be. As you can tell from my story about failing algebra in public school, I wasn't very good at being someone other than myself either. I couldn't figure out how to balance my family responsibilities with being my true self. I was overcorrecting my personality, and it was bad for me.

Sometimes our parents, teachers, and friends expect us to fill certain roles. A lot of the time, we're afraid we can't live up to their expectations. We don't want to take on the responsibilities they give to us in case the people we admire the most will reject us. Sometimes the stakes are incredibly high. Striving to please others is stressful, especially when we have to shut down parts of our own personalities to give people what they expect.

If people in your family tell you to do something, you usually don't have a lot of room to say no. Most of the time, your family will tell you they have your best interests at heart, and that they're only trying to teach you how to be a responsible adult who follows through on commitments. It's usually no big deal to take out the trash or babysit a younger sibling, but sometimes your responsibilities amount to much more than a few chores. While it's always important to practice your responsibility, it's crushing when it gets to be so much that you feel like you don't control your own life.

There are several things you can do to level with your parents. The best-case scenario is that they simply want you to help out with something or be involved in an activity that you get to choose. If they don't like the activity you've chosen, compromise by letting them pick one activity and letting you pick a different one.

If your parents are trying to teach you responsibility by forcing you to do something you don't want to do, suggest a similar activity that interests you more. If they want you to help out around the house, suggest some chores you don't mind doing so you aren't stuck with the ones you hate. If they want you to join a sport, try convincing them to let you choose the sport. Brainstorm ways to come to an agreement so you don't feel like you're living their life and not your own. Then, once you've committed to something, do your best to show your parents that you really mean to follow through. You'll earn their trust, and they'll be more likely to ease up on their level of control once they see you mean business.

If all else fails, remember that the things your parents want you to do are temporary. There will come a time where you get to decide everything. Until then, maybe you can find something you like about the responsibilities that you have.

Even though I didn't like how constricted I was by my family's social life at church, I'm proud of how those responsibilities turned me into a compassionate person. I know what it's like to feel like you're on the other side, like you don't fit in. I've spent a lot of time feeling bad about myself, so I feel for other people who do too. My compassion fuels my passion—that's why I do what I do. That's why I'm writing this book: to tell other girls like me that they aren't alone and things will get better. I know I can't fix people, but I can give them hope.

There's also no rule that says you can't follow your

passions outside of the responsibilities your parents assign. When I was a kid, I loved to sing. I sang in my room all the time when nobody was around, and it brought me a lot of joy. Giving yourself small moments of joy or peace helps you conquer all the tasks at hand.

Remember that the responsibilities that pay off for us in the long run are the ones that align with our values. To be authentic to what you love, a brainstorming session is a great place to start. Think about what you're doing when you're happiest. Think about problems in the world or the community that you care about and how you could help create positive change. Think about the people you admire and why. These can all guide you to activities that DO make you feel good, and activities that could lead to lifelong passions.

I AM A RESCUER.

I will be a leader.

Taking on responsibility to really go after what you want gives you enormous power not only in your own life, but as a leader and inspiration to others. Responsibility is a process that starts with you, and then it snowballs into effects that seem bigger than you had originally hoped. That's because those grand success stories we all admire weren't usually built from one giant heroic action, but from a lot of smaller battles fought over and over again. The changemakers of the world know that doing small tasks consistently is how you build the big impact of your dreams.

We often hear stories about high achievers who practiced their passion for twelve hours a day. The stories of our idols sweating away the days and nights to viciously achieve are everywhere. We love a good story of someone who never gives up and goes to great lengths to be the best. But getting to your goals isn't usually a mad sprint. The goal is to do something you're passionate about consistently over time. When you first start out, don't pressure yourself to work twelve hours a day. The whole goal of remaining responsible to a passion is to grow a life that you enjoy. If you put too much pressure on yourself to perform at superhuman levels all the time, you can lose your enjoyment for the things you care about most.

The beginning of the process to achieve your dreams is simply about making that first small commitment to something you really like and sticking with it. This stage is about having fun with something and exploring it in depth. It can be easy at first, because we do things that interest us all the time for fun. The beginning is an exciting time when the possibilities seem endless because you haven't yet faced a huge challenge. Maybe it's the first time you played basketball before you joined the team. Maybe it's the little movie you made on your dad's camera before you started your first YouTube channel. Maybe it's the short story you wrote in your journal before you began sharing your writing with others, or the science project you did in your kitchen before you ever began to compete in regional contests.

As you continue exploring what you love, some of the initial energy you had can seem to wear off. After all, it's one thing to make one short movie, and quite another thing to spend several hours a week doing those things for years. Your first short story may fly onto the page without you thinking much about it. But when you do something for a long time, you're bound to have days when you aren't inspired. These are the times when it's most import-ant to not give up. These setbacks and failures are the most important times in the story of you and your passion, because that's when you get to define the kind of person you truly are.

Be Resilient

When we think about the people we admire, it's easy to believe those people were always amazing. We imagine that they had firey talent from day one, and that every day after that was a straight shoot to the top. Our heroes make things look so effortless that it's hard to imagine them as anything other than what we see on the surface.

But the truth is that nobody achieves anything without setbacks. Our heroes became the great peo-ple they are because they didn't let one failure bring them down. They didn't let the word "no" stop them from achieving their dreams. They decided it was more important to do something they valued than to listen to the little voice in the back of their head telling them one failure meant they would never succeed. People who live their dreams know failure happens all the time; and although it doesn't feel great, it also doesn't define us and our capabilities. Overcoming failures to keep working toward your goals and dreams is what it means to be resilient.

I don't know anybody who has gotten to a place of success without some kind of setback or stressful event. Those growing pains present us with opportunities to change or to stay the same, but we don't come out unscathed. When we experience setbacks, it's okay to feel negative emotions; we don't need to bounce back right away. But it's more important to see that every setback is just one small moment in the larger story of our lives. When we're right in the middle of the letdown, it's hard to feel like things will ever get better or that we'll ever overcome them. But those moments don't last, and they can help us define the direction we want to take moving forward.

I grew up with a lot of emotional struggles in my life, so one of my personal meters of success is building healthy relationships with people. Having people who love you for who you are and who make you feel safe is hard! When I was twenty, I thought I had finally found someone like that in my boyfriend at the time.

We had been dating for a year and a half, and my boyfriend had become very close with my family. I was starting to trust him, which was a big deal—I had stopped trusting most boys ever since my high-school boyfriend cheated on me. All my boyfriends before had made me feel like I was never enough, but this one made me feel like I was actually *too much* and he loved me for it anyway. I was so much to handle, though, that he said no one else would ever put up with me like he did. That's the kind of back-handed compliment that sounds nice on the surface but is actually cruel underneath—and I liked him so much that I was only letting myself see things as they were on the surface.

Whenever my boyfriend was around while my family and I were arguing or having unpleasant conversations, I trusted that he would never share that information with other people. (Remember: because of my dad's position in the church, we weren't allowed to be imperfect and get into the occasional normal, healthy spat.) But as it turned out, these family secrets weren't safe with my boyfriend. He worked at a barbershop, and he was telling everyone there about what was going on with my family.

From there, the rumors spread like oil in the community. I was so sick about his betrayal of my trust that it got to the point where I collapsed from anxiety again. I still didn't know I had anxiety then, but I knew this response wasn't normal.

My boyfriend apologized, and I could tell he felt bad for what he did. I decided to forgive him and stay together. He had done such a good job of convincing me that I'd never find anyone else to love me the way he did, so I felt like leaving him wasn't an option. It's easy to make bad decisions like this when you don't feel good about yourself. Choosing to forgive and stay with him was a huge setback on my path to discovering my true self-worth.

After that, though, I never looked at him the same way again. Things didn't go back to normal between us, and we ended things a couple of months later. When we broke up, I knew things had to change. I couldn't keep dating guys who made me feel like I was lucky to be with them when they were the ones lucky to be with *me*. This breakup was a turning point in my journey to finding healthy love, because I started telling myself after that point that I deserved better. There were other guys in the world, and I didn't have to stay with one who treated me poorly. I was going to commit to myself over anyone who didn't treat me well, and I was going to set my goals on finding the kind of unfamiliar love that we talked about in chapter 5.

Not that I got it right the first time after that. I had to keep reminding myself I deserved better. The path to success isn't linear—it comes with setbacks and missteps. That's how you learn, and that's how you earn your success. Whether your goal is something tangible (like winning a basketball tournament) or conceptual (like building great love and friendships), the challenges you face on the road to victory are what make the journey a valuable life experience.

Give It Time

The actions we take day after day to pursue our dreams will always make those times of struggle worth it in the long run. When we commit to something we care about with consistent action over time, it doesn't matter what level we started at because we'll naturally improve. After all, how could you do something over and over and NOT get better?

Consistent effort is how people become masters

in their art. They get into something because they enjoy doing it, and then they continue to learn and grow. They ask what they could do differently next time to be better. They ask what other information they need to help them improve. Over many practices, they become better until, one day, they become good. Then, with some more time and effort, they become outstanding. Eventually they become masters. It all happened because they continued to stay passionate and to learn and grow. They took their strengths and built them up to incredible heights. But they did it all with patience, because they knew it would take time.

When you build your skill set in a certain area, people will notice. Teachers will feel motivated by a young person taking charge of their destiny, and more likely than not, one of them will give you a helping hand. These are people who could help you get into your dream college, recommend you for cool opportunities, and get your work noticed by other people who can help you make your dreams come true.

Throughout the process of building up your skill set, you'll find new friends who have the same passions you do. They may become friends you can collaborate with on projects or talk to about the things that matter to you most. They can also inspire you during those times when you're feeling down and help you get back on your feet again.

Responsibility to your passion brings fulfillment, community, and confidence. It can launch you into the next step of your life, and each step after that. Eventually it can make you a master of your craft and a changemaker who is an inspiration to others. You'll feel like you're living a life of value because you committed yourself to something you thought was important and you watched yourself get better. You'll become the leader you always looked up to.

I AM A TRAILBLAZER.

I will be my own role model.

It can be hard to remain true to the commitments that matter to you, especially when so many other people tell you what responsibilities you should take seriously. You may be in a situation where you don't have a strong role model or someone to cheer you on as you achieve what matters to you. Your friends may be struggling with their own issues and unable to be supportive. When you stick with the things that matter most to you, you're being true to yourself, and that can get lonely. But that's what makes you a trailblazer: you're becoming your own role model, and a role model to the other people in your life.

Everyone needs a role model—someone who can inspire us to grow and change for the better, someone who can mentor us in making hard choices, someone who can show us what our futures could look like. We compare ourselves to our role models in ways that make us want to become better people, not in ways that make us hate ourselves. Even role models have role models! They can be a parent, teacher, coach, therapist, activist, athlete—the list goes on.

Being your own role model is scary, which is why it helps to have other people to look up to. I've always looked up to Harriet Tubman. She's my hero and role model because she put herself at risk to help others—but she didn't do it until after she had saved herself first. Once she was free from slavery, and when she tasted freedom and learned what it was all about, she went back for other people so they could experience it too. She was probably scared, but she did it anyway. She probably wanted to quit, but she did it anyway. That's what makes her a trailblazer.

I feel that way too, and I know there are other people at stake besides myself. I'm a role model because I know what it's like to be an outsider. I don't preach higher than I live—I walk the walk, and I talk the talk. I'll tell you how it is according to my opinion, and I live by that to the best of my ability. I'm willing to put myself out there as much as possible for the benefit of anyone else—and I'm so determined to make it better for them, especially other girls like me.

Being a role model means you're committed to being your authentic self, even when it's hard. It means doing what you know is right and doing the most good you can do, even when you feel like you're the only one doing it. You may not always feel like people are watching what you do, but how you act when you think no one is watching says more about you than anything else.

Sometimes it doesn't feel like being responsible to your values or a role model is worth it. It may make you feel lonely, especially when you're surrounded by other people who seem like they're all connected. But if you don't believe in the values that guide those people, hanging out with them is only going to make you uncomfortable. You deserve to be around people who are on your wavelength, not with people who make you feel bad.

Here's the cool thing: once you start being your authentic, self-loving self, you'll start to attract the kind of friends who are also authentic and self-loving and who love you for who you are too. Suddenly you aren't alone anymore. You've built a support network around you that's always there to remind yourself of all the goodness you deserve. Those kinds of friends are the people we know we can keep our commitments to, because being around them is fun and easy. Those are the people who will support us to be who we truly are.

It takes a lot of courage to step forward and try to honestly go after the life we want for ourselves. Let your previous achievements drive you forward, even if it's just that one afternoon you decided you were going to practice doing something you love. Know that you have the power to change your life for the better and to create positive change for other people too. Respect the person you are, and allow yourself to see everything in you that's good, strong, and brave. You have everything you need to be the role model you always wanted for yourself—and more.

MENTAL HEALTH AT A GLANCE

Depression

Depression is one of the most common mental health disorders. Two of its most prominent types include major (or clinical) depression and bipolar disorder. In general, people who experience depression feel an overwhelming sense of sadness or numbness that continues for weeks on end. They tend to feel isolated from other people, even when they're in the same room with family or friends. They aren't interested in the world around them or the things they used to really enjoy. They believe they are worthless, that people don't see them for who they truly are, and that people would be better off without them. In severe cases, depressed people may want to commit suicide or harm themselves.

People with bipolar disorder have time periods where they feel depressed, and time periods where they feel manic. If depression includes feeling unmotivated, worthless, and numb, manic episodes are almost the opposite. Someone in a manic episode feels like they have an abundance of energy. They feel super happy and motivated, like they could take on the world. Sometimes they don't sleep very much, their thoughts race, and their activity increases. Most people don't experience such high levels of energy in their day-to-day lives. This surge of energy comes before a crash, where the bipolar person goes back to being depressed again.

Major (Clinical) Depression Symptoms

- Feelings of sadness, anger, hopelessness, loneliness, and/or irritability

- Difficulty paying attention during school and/or completing homework and other chores

- Excessive sleepiness, difficulty sleeping, or sleeping more than usual

- Changes in appetite, either eating significantly more or less than normal

- Loss of interest in people and activities that once brought you joy

- Thoughts of suicide and/or self-harm

Bipolar Disorder Symptoms

- Feelings and behavior swing between symptoms of major depression (above) and manic episodes

- Manic symptoms include:

  » Feeling abnormally energetic, active, or wired

  » Not needing as much sleep as usual

  » Talking fast or more than normal, and/or having rapid thoughts

  » Being easily distracted

  » Making reckless decisions, or decisions you wouldn't normally make

Anxiety

Dealing with panic attacks and feeling constantly on edge and worried can leave you feeling drained and unable to cope with the next day. The state of racing thoughts and constant panic can make it hard to socialize and go to school. After all, when you're constantly imagining everything that could go wrong, it's hard to feel optimistic about the things that could go right. Anxiety—which doctors call generalized anxiety disorder—makes it hard for people to enjoy the present moment. While it's normal to feel nervous in certain situations like before a test or a speech, when you have anxiety, you might feel nervous in all kinds of situations, like before you hang out with your friends or when you're doing your math homework. That constant, high-level sense of nervousness can make your interactions with other people tiring. Someone with an anxiety disorder might also feel anxious about their anxiety itself because they're worried other people will judge them for it. This becomes an exhausting loop of worry that takes someone away from themselves.

Generalized Anxiety Disorder Symptoms

- Frequent worry about school, activities, being on time, the safety of your family and friends, or the possibility of natural disasters or other uncontrollable events

- Constant need for perfectionism or to redo things until they are perfect

- Requiring lots of approval or reassurance from others that you are doing things right

- Lacking confidence at school and in other social situations

- Frequent stomachaches, indigestion problems, or other physical aches and pains

ADHD

Being a girl with ADHD (attention deficit/hyperactivity disorder) is tough. Some people believe young boys are commonly overdiagnosed with ADHD to conveniently excuse their parents for being blamed for not teaching them good manners. Girls are expected to be a lot more composed and obedient than boys, so when girls *do* need treatment for ADHD, they aren't taken seriously.

Girls also present ADHD differently than boys. Whereas boys often present ADHD by being loud and obnoxious, girls are often taught shame about their symptoms and try to channel them into behaviors that might seem outwardly productive or non-disruptive, but aren't at all. For example, they might find a lot of excuses to get up multiple times during one class to sharpen their pencil, throw something away, open and close a window, or perform other nonobtrusive behaviors. When girls with ADHD sit down to do their homework, they can commonly struggle to focus on one assignment at a time. Instead, they might start three things at once and get too overwhelmed to finish any of them.

ADHD Symptoms

- Difficulty focusing during class, while doing homework or reading, or in other situations that require sitting still and paying attention

- Struggling to complete tasks, and often abandoning them before they are done

- Performing tasks in a very inefficient way

- Frequently losing things or forgetting about responsibilities

- Fidgeting a lot and being easily distracted

- Talking excessively or interrupting others when they talk

PTSD

PTSD (post-traumatic stress disorder) affects people who have lived through traumatic experiences. They may have suffered from abuse, witnessed or experienced violence, or been in a terrible accident. They frequently have experiences where they vividly relive the traumatic thing that happened to them as if it were happening all over again. PTSD can come with unpredictable panic attacks. A person with PTSD might constantly think about what they would do if such a terrible thing were to happen again and react strongly to things that remind them of their traumatic experience. Certain places or people could remind them of that trauma, and it may be impossible for them to see those people or go to those places without experiencing severe anxiety. They could move through the world with a heightened sense of awareness, where they constantly take stock of who and what is around them. PTSD can be an all-consuming experience that alters a person's ability to lead a life free from worry.

PTSD Symptoms

- Frequent upsetting flashbacks, memories, or dreams of the traumatic event

- Avoiding things related to that event, such as people, locations, or activities

- Reenacting the event while playing games

- Symptoms of major depression (see page 156) and/or ADHD (see page 160):

  » Feelings of sadness, worthlessness, irritability, or guilt

  » Fidgeting or trouble focusing

  » Difficulty falling or staying asleep, or sleeping more than normal

  » Thoughts of suicide and/or self-harm

Eating Disorders

Eating disorders look different from person to person, and you do not have to look a certain way to have one. People with anorexia nervosa often eat dangerously little and sometimes obsessively exercise and track their food. Another common eating disorder is bulimia nervosa, where someone goes through cycles of dieting, binging, and purging. Binge-eating disorder is similar, but without the obsessive cycles of purging or cataloging food intake. Binging is when someone eats significantly more food than a normal serving size, and they don't necessarily stop once they are full. Eating disorders are driven by shame about your body as much as they are about seeking comfort and control over yourself and your life—it is common for people with eating disorders to also have other mental health struggles, such as depression.

Anorexia Symptoms

- Limiting food intake to an extreme, dangerous degree

- Obsessively counting and tracking calories and food intake, sometimes in a food journal

- Overexercising to burn off calorie intake, and/or binging and purging eating patterns

- Intense fear of gaining weight, and/or low self-esteem about your body image

- Distorted body image, such as seeing yourself as overweight even if you are visibly underweight

- Being severely underweight for your age and height

Bulimia Symptoms

- Repeatedly binging on large amounts of food and feeling out of control in your consumption

- Purging afterward via vomiting, exercising, or using laxatives

- Intentionally purging at least once a week for an extended period of time

- Severely limiting food intake between binging sessions

- Intense fear of gaining weight, and/or low self-esteem about your body image

Binge-Eating Disorder Symptoms

- Repeatedly binging on large amounts of food and feeling out of control in your consumption

- Eating even if you are not hungry, and/or until you are uncomfortably full

- Hiding your eating behavior from others, and feeling shame or guilt about your intake

- Not using any form of calorie restriction or purging behaviors

- Frequently claiming to go on a diet without ever seeing results

RESOURCES

Hotlines

Crisis Text Line
Text: HOME to 741741
www.crisistextline.org

NAMI (National Alliance on Mental Illness) Helpline
Call: 1-800-950-6264
www.nami.org

National Runaway Safeline
Call: 1-800-786-2929
Text: 66008
www.1800runaway.org

National Sexual Assault Hotline
Call: 1-800-656-4673
www.rainn.org

National Suicide Prevention Lifeline
Call: 1-800-273-8255
www.suicidepreventionlifeline.org

SAMHSA (Substance Abuse and Mental Health Services Administration) National Helpline
Call: 1-800-662-4357
www.samhsa.gov

Trans Lifeline Hotline
Call: 1-877-565-8860
www.translifeline.org

The Trevor Project Lifeline
Call: 1-866-488-7386
Text: 678-678
www.thetrevorproject.org

Organizations & Websites

Black Female Therapists
Instagram: @blackfemaletherapists
www.blackfemaletherapists.com

Black Mental Wellness
Instagram: @blackmentalwellness
www.blackmentalwellness.com

Brown Girl Self-Care
Instagram: @browngirlselfcare
www.browngirlselfcare.com

Sad Girls Club
Instagram: @sadgirlsclub
www.sadgirlsclub.org

Therapy for Black Girls
Instagram: @therapyforblackgirls
www.therapyforblackgirls.com

Books

Becoming by Michelle Obama

Body Kindness: Transform Your Health from the Inside Out—and Never Say Diet Again by Rebecca Scritchfield

The Gifts of Imperfection: Let Go of Who You Think You're Supposed to Be and Embrace Who You Are by Brené Brown

The Happiness Project: Or, Why I Spent a Year Trying to Sing in the Morning, Clean My Closets, Fight Right, Read Aristotle, and Generally Have More Fun by Gretchen Rubin

Introvert Power: Why Your Inner Life Is Your Hidden Strength by Laurie Helgoe, PhD

Intuitive Eating: A Revolutionary Anti-Diet Approach
by Evelyn Tribole

Letting Go of Leo: How I Broke Up with Perfection
by Simi Botic

Podcasts

Balanced Black Girl
Instagram: @balancedblackgirlpodcast
www.balancedblackgirl.com/category/podcast

Black Girls Heal
Facebook: @blackgirlheal
Instagram: @blackgirlsheal_
www.podcasts.apple.com/us/podcast/black-girls-heal/id1448286071

Brown Girl Self-Care
www.browngirlselfcare.com/podcast-1

hey, girl.
Instagram: @theheygirlpodcast
cms.megaphone.fm/channel/heygirl

Therapy for Black Girls
www.therapyforblackgirls.com/podcast

Apps & Instagram Accounts

Calm app
Instagram: @calm
www.calm.com

Hi Anxiety
Instagram: @_hi_anxiety_

Talkspace app
Instagram: @talkspace
www.talkspace.com

In early 2016, Achea Redd was diagnosed with generalized anxiety disorder. After hiding her condition out of fear and shame, Achea quickly realized it was only getting worse, affecting her physically to the point of a nervous breakdown. It wasn't until she acknowledged the situation with her loved ones, seeking out treatment from her therapist and doctor, that things started to get better.

As a form of self-expression and healing, Achea created her own blog, sharing her feelings about mental health and authenticity. The flow of support she received from the community compelled her to create Real Girls FART—a space to empower and equip women with the necessary tools to use their voices and become their best, most authentic selves. Achea currently resides in Columbus, Ohio, with her husband, Michael, and her two children.